Essential Histories

The Korean War 1950–1953

Carter Malkasian

OSPREY
PUBLISHING

First published in Great Britain in 2001 by Osprey Publishing,
Elms Court, Chapel Way, Botley, Oxford OX2 9LP

Email: info@ospreypublishing.com

ISBN 1 84176 282 2

Editor: Rebecca Cullen
Design: Ken Vail Graphic Design, Cambridge, UK
Cartography by The Map Studio
Index by Susan Williams
Picture research by Image Select International
Origination by Grasmere Digital Imaging, Leeds, UK
Printed and bound in China by L. Rex Printing Company Ltd

01 02 03 04 05   10 9 8 7 6 5 4 3 2 1

For a complete list of titles available from Osprey Publishing
please contact:

Osprey Direct UK, PO Box 140,
Wellingborough, Northants, NN8 4ZA, UK
Email: info@ospreydirect.co.uk

Osprey Direct USA,
c/o Motorbooks International, PO Box 1,
Osceola, WI 54020-0001, USA.
Email: info@ospreydirectusa.com

www.ospreypublishing.com

KEY TO MILITARY SYMBOLS

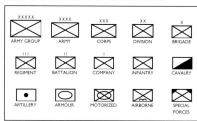

Essential Histories

The Korean War 1950–1953

Contents

Introduction

From 1950 to 1953, the most powerful countries in the world engaged in a major conventional war on the Korean peninsula. Arguably, the world has never been so close to a third World War, not even during the Cuban Missile Crisis. At times, both combatants thought the war was a preamble to a much larger and more destructive global conflict. It was the only occasion in the Cold War when the military forces of the People's Republic of China (PRC), the Soviet Union, and the USA (plus its Western allies) met in combat. On the ground, Chinese armies engaged in huge battles with the American-led United Nations Command (UNC). In the air, hundreds of Soviet, Chinese, and American jet aircraft fought for air supremacy over North Korea. Thus, the Korean War was not merely a war fought between proxies of the major powers, like the later conflicts in Vietnam or Afghanistan, but a much more significant conflagration. The war changed how the East and the West dealt with one another and was part of a revolution in the conduct of war.

The Korean War was a conflict over two prizes: first, political control of Korea; and second, power in east Asia and the world as a whole. Historically, Communists and right-wing Nationalists vied for political control of Korea. Following the Second World War, the Communists gained control of North Korea and rightists gained control of South Korea. Both then wanted to unify the entire peninsula under their respective authority. This was what motivated North Korea to invade South Korea in June 1950. However, Korea was also an object of Cold War superpower competition. After 1945 the USA was the dominant power in the Pacific. The other superpower, the Soviet Union, led by the paranoid Josef Stalin, was cautiously seeking to expand its global power by promoting Communism in regions important to its security. Korea was one of those areas. The Soviet Union and the PRC believed that a Communist Korea provided insurance against American aggression; hence the Soviet Union's backing of the North Korean invasion and China's later intervention in the war. The USA reacted to the North Korean invasion as a threat to its influence in east Asia. More broadly, American leaders believed that if the invasion were not confronted, the Soviets would be encouraged to engage in military expansionism elsewhere in the world.

The course of the Korean War can be divided into two periods, one of maneuver and one of attrition. The first six months of the war was a period of maneuver. First, North Korea invaded most of South Korea in a blitzkrieg assault on 25 June 1950. Next, US General Douglas MacArthur conducted a brilliant amphibious attack at Inchon and drove the North Koreans out of South Korea. Then, threatened by the UNC advance into North Korea, the PRC intervened and pressed the UNC back into South Korea. Instead of unifying Korea or ending the war, each of these decisive victories led to an escalation of the war. To prevent the conflict from spiralling into a Third World War, the USA abandoned its goal of attaining a total victory and decided to fight a limited war in December 1950.

The remainder of the war, from 1951 to 1953, was marked by indecisive attrition. The UNC's object was to hold the Communists on the battlefield while seeking a resolution of the conflict based not on unifying Korea, but on preserving the integrity of South Korea. The Communists agreed to negotiations following the defeat of their Fifth Phase Offensive in June 1951. Negotiations proceeded slowly because neither side wanted to compromise on issues like the location of the cease-fire line and the fate of the prisoners of war. Military operations continued in the form of limited attacks, air-to-air battles, and strategic bombing campaigns. An armistice was finally concluded on 27 July

1953 after the Chinese and North Korean economies could no longer support war, the USA was threatening to escalate the conflict, and Stalin had died.

Ironically, the Korean War is well known as the USA's 'Forgotten War.' This is because it does not figure nearly as highly in the national consciousness as the Second World War, the Vietnam War, or the 1991 Gulf War. One reason that the Korean War has been 'forgotten' is that, with the exception of the Inchon landing, it seems boring and featureless. However, there are actually several major battles that were as important as Inchon, if not more so. Two stand out in particular. First, the initial Chinese intervention in the war in November 1950 resulted in the resounding defeat of the UNC and the longest retreat in American military history. The ensuing panic amongst American leaders nearly caused them to take actions that probably would have led to a Third World War. Second, the Communists suffered an even worse defeat when the UNC crushed their Fifth Phase Offensive in April and May 1951. This was a turning point in the war, the Communists being forced to abandon their quest to unify Korea and accept that the war would end through compromise.

Besides battles, there are a number of generals in the Korean War who should not be forgotten. MacArthur is obviously massively important. His brilliant victory at Inchon and his later dismissal have made him a magnetic historical figure. The decisive strategies that he espoused are a rallying point for those who agree that the only aim in war should be total victory. But MacArthur was outshone in nearly every respect by his subordinate and later successor, General Matthew Ridgway. His dynamic leadership revitalized the defeated Eighth US Army and prevented the Communists from capturing South Korea. Ridgway understood that, in the Cold War, seeking total victory was an outmoded military strategy. Therefore, he developed an operational doctrine of attrition that did not result in escalation, yet enforced the UNC bargaining position in negotiations. Two other generals are worthy of note. The young South Korean, General Paik Sun Yup, won several victories

with his underequipped men and was instrumental in modernizing the army of the Republic of Korea (ROK). On the Communist side, the innovative and insightful General Deng Hua reformed the Chinese forces in Korea, known as the Chinese People's Volunteers (CPV), into a modern army capable of holding its own against the UNC.

Historically, the Korean War was a significant turning point in the Cold War. This conflict in a small peninsula in east Asia affected the entire international system and the balance of power between the two superpowers. Through the conflict, the West demonstrated its resolve to thwart Communist aggression. The USA and its allies strengthened NATO and took steps to defend their interests throughout the world. The conflict convinced the American leadership of the need to engage in a massive rearmament, setting the tone for the arms races that marked the remainder of the Cold War. The Korean War also marked the rise of China as a military power. After the impressive performance of the CPV, the USA was forced to treat the PRC as a major power in east Asia. In general, the UNC success in the Korean War probably deterred China and the Soviet Union from instigating further conventional wars against the West or its interests.

Finally, the Korean War defined the new strategic context of warfare that emerged in the Cold War. Wars were conducted in an entirely new manner. Before 1945, the aims of most wars had been total victory: the annihilation of an opponent. After 1945, the advent of nuclear weapons and the increasing power of conventional weapons made total war prohibitively dangerous. The risk of mutual destruction could not be countenanced. Instead of total victory, limited aims were now sought in most wars. In turn, the means of warfare became more limited as careful measures were taken to reduce the risk of a conflict escalating into a Third World War. The Korean War was the first example of such a limited war. The strategies and operational doctrines employed were the first adaptations to limited war. As such, the Korean War was the formative experience in the strategy and operational techniques developed during the Cold War.

Chronology

1950 25 June North Korea invades South Korea
7 July UN Security Council creates the United Nations Command
1 August–22 September Battles around the Pusan Perimeter
15 September Inchon landing
2 October Chairman Mao Zedong decides that China will intervene in the war
7 October American forces cross the 38th Parallel
15 October President Harry Truman and General Douglas MacArthur meet on Wake Island
27 October–2 November Communist First Phase Offensive
25 November–9 December Communist Second Phase Offensive
27 November–25 December Battle of the Chosin Reservoir
8 December Truman–Attlee communiqué
23 December General Matthew Ridgway is appointed commander of the Eighth Army
31 December–24 January Communist Third Phase Offensive
1951 25 January–11 February Operation Thunderbolt
11–18 February Communist Fourth Phase Offensive
14 March Eighth Army recaptures Seoul
11 April Truman dismisses MacArthur; Ridgway replaces him
22 April–20 May Communist Fifth Phase Offensive
23 June Soviet Ambassador to the UN, Jakob Malik, proposes cease-fire negotiations
10 July Cease-fire negotiations open at Kaesong

23 August Communists suspend cease-fire negotiations over alleged UNC violation of the neutral zone around Kaesong
3–18 October Operation Commando
25 October Truce talks resume at new neutral site of Panmunjom
27 November Agreement reached on the location of a cease-fire line
1952 8 April Screening begins of Communist prisoners of war
7 May Brigadier General Dodd is seized in Koje-do prison riots
12 May General Mark Clark replaces Ridgway as commander of the UNC
24 May Rhee declares martial law in South Korean temporary capital, Pusan
23 June Air strikes against North Korean hydroelectric plants
11 July First strike on Pyongyang
29 August Second strike on Pyongyang, the largest bombing raid of the war
8 October Clark recesses cease-fire negotiations indefinitely
4 November Dwight Eisenhower is elected President of the United States
1953 5 March Death of Josef Stalin
28 March Zhou Enlai accepts 'Little Switch'
26 April Cease-fire negotiations resume
13 May Beginning of UNC air strikes on North Korean dams
25 May UNC delegation presents its 'final position'
10–16 June Communists assault the II ROK Corps in the Kumsong bulge
16 June First cease-fire concluded
18 June Rhee unilaterally releases 25,000 North Korean prisoners of war
13–27 July Final Communist offensive
27 July The UNC and the Communists sign the armistice, ending hostilities

Two Koreas, the Superpowers, and China

The Korean War took place in two different contexts: the superpower competition of the Cold War and the regional competition for political control of Korea. Both are important to understanding the motivations of the warring parties.

The Cold War

After the Second World War, the USA and the Soviet Union were the two remaining truly great powers. Their interests began to clash as each asserted its influence over the postwar world. This competition had a deep ideological tone. The USA and its allies, collectively known as the West, promoted democracy and capitalism, while the Soviet Union and its supporters sought to expand Communism. With the declaration of the

Truman Doctrine in 1947, the USA adopted a policy of containment: opposing Communist expansion where it threatened the development of democracy. In 1948, the North Atlantic Treaty Organization (NATO) was established to defend Western Europe against Soviet aggression. Nevertheless, until June 1950 the degree of the Soviet threat was unclear. Therefore, the West had not undertaken significant military preparations to confront Soviet or Communist expansionism. NATO was only a skeletal organization without the conventional and nuclear strength that would be associated with it later in the Cold War. The American armed forces were also in a low state of readiness. Following demobilization after the Second World War, the Republican Congress had drastically cut American defense expenditure, pegging at less than 3 percent of the gross domestic product (GDP).

The Cold War represented a new military situation as well as a new international one. After 1945, warfare underwent a revolution. Before 1945, most wars had been fought with the goal of decisively annihilating an enemy's armed forces. Warfare continued until one side unconditionally surrendered. After 1945, such total warfare became prohibitively costly. There were three basic reasons for this. First, the advent of atomic weapons multiplied the destructiveness of warfare. Seeking a total victory became a very dangerous endeavor when an opponent might use atomic or nuclear weapons if faced with a major defeat on the battlefield. Second, the First and Second World Wars

US President Harry Truman. Truman implemented the Truman Doctrine, which stated that the USA would oppose aggression against democratic countries. This was the basis of the containment policy that guided American diplomacy through the Cold War. (Ann Ronan Picture Library)

showed that conventional warfare itself was an exhausting affair. In 1950, the Soviet Union, Japan, China, and Europe had not yet fully recovered from the world wars and lacked the economic strength to enter another one. Third, the bipolar nature of the international system meant that even peripheral conflicts were often the concern of the superpowers. Any gain by one superpower was a loss for the other. Therefore, there was a risk that any conflict involving a superpower or one of its allies could escalate into a Third World War.

The Korean peninsula

From 1905 to 1945, Korea was under the control of Japan. During this time, Koreans fervently sought to form their own nation-state. Unfortunately, Communists and rightists disputed who would rule an independent Korea. The Korean Communist

movement conducted a low-level guerrilla war against the Japanese. Meanwhile, exiled non-Communist Koreans formed a Nationalist provisional government in Shanghai. Dr Syngman Rhee was a South Korean leader who, for a brief period in the early 1920s, was president of the provisional government. During the Second World War, Rhee lived in the USA, where he vociferously condemned Japan. His actions earned him popular recognition in Korea.

US President Franklin Roosevelt wanted to place Korea under international trusteeship once Japan was defeated. At the Tehran Conference in 1943, the Soviet Union, the UK, and the USA agreed that Korea should be run under an international trusteeship before becoming fully independent. However, the details of trusteeship were not determined before the Soviet Red Army annihilated the Japanese army in Manchuria and pressed into Korea in August 1945. Stalin agreed to divide Korea with the USA

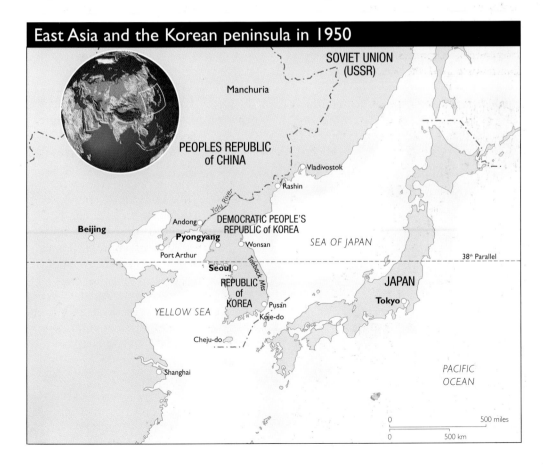

East Asia and the Korean peninsula in 1950

along the arbitrary line of the 38th Parallel. The bulk of the Korean population as well as the capital city of Seoul fell into the American zone. The northern industrial half of Korea went to the Soviets.

At the end of the Second World War, the USA was the dominant power in east Asia. Having fought the Pacific War to eliminate Japanese economic and military strength, the USA now considered the entire Pacific Ocean to be its sphere of influence. However, American leaders were unsure of how Korea fell into this sphere of influence. Many, including the supreme commander in the Far East, General Douglas MacArthur, believed that Korea was irrelevant.

The domestic political scene in Korea was turbulent as rightists and Communists vied for power. General John Hodge was commander of the American occupational zone. Extremely anti-Communist, Hodge first relied on the Japanese police and administrators to run South Korea. The Shanghai government was disregarded. Rightists like Rhee appealed to Hodge for support, which he readily gave.

The Soviets unsurprisingly supported the development of Communism in North Korea. Their interest in Korea derived from their desire to maintain a sphere of influence in east Asia. Stalin did not want Korea to become a staging ground for an invasion of the Soviet Union. However, control of all of Korea could not easily be attained in the midst of American hegemony over the Pacific. Stalin was not ready to risk a major conflict and preferred to protect Soviet security by establishing North Korea as a buffer. The Soviets and Korean Communists purged all non-Communists from leadership positions in North Korea. The North Korean Communist Party was officially formed in July 1946. With Soviet support, Kim Il Sung established authority over other prominent figures within the party. Kim had been trained by the Soviet Union and, in the Second World War, had fought the Japanese as a guerrilla in Manchuria. With these developments, North Korea was progressing toward cohesive statehood.

At the Moscow Conference in December 1945, the USA and the Soviet Union made an agreement on the future of Korea. Their

North Korean leader Kim Il Sung (left) and Chinese Premier Zhou Enlai (right) at a cocktail party. Kim Il Sung was the main advocate for invading South Korea. Zhou was the PRC's number one diplomat. He conducted most of the negotiations with the Soviet Union regarding China's entry into the war. (China Photo Service/Eastphoto)

respective occupational commands would form a joint commission to advise on the formation of a provisional government. Trusteeship would occur after a provisional government had been established. The agreement suited Soviet interests because it stipulated that the new government must be amenable to the Soviet Union. The South Korean people were hostile to the agreement. They opposed trusteeship of any sort. The first meeting of the joint commission was held between March and May 1946. It dealt with the identification of Korean groups that could be approached for the eventual formation of a government. The Soviets refused to recognize groups that rejected the 1945 Moscow Conference agreement, meaning nearly every important South Korean political party. Disagreement could not be overcome and the commission adjourned to resume its debate the following year. When the joint commission reconvened in May 1947, proceedings quickly became bogged down over the same issues. In September, the USA decided to hand the problem of Korea over to the United Nations (UN).

In September 1947, the US Joint Chiefs of Staff (JCS) assessed that the USA had little interest in maintaining troops and bases in Korea. In April 1948, the National Security Council (NSC) recommended withdrawing American military forces but providing military and economic aid to bolster South Korea's security. President Harry Truman adopted this recommendation even though it failed to address how the USA should respond to overt Communist aggression. US troop withdrawal began on 19 May 1948.

Meanwhile, in November 1947, the UN General Assembly recognized Korea's right to independence and established a commission to supervise elections, the United Nations Temporary Commission on Korea (UNTCOK). The elections were intended to create a constituent assembly that would unify the nation prior to the withdrawal of foreign occupation forces. The resolution passed over the objection of the Soviet Union. Consequently, the Soviets would not allow UNTCOK to enter North Korea. Nevertheless,

the USA secured UN authorization for UNTCOK to supervise elections solely in the South for a 'National Government' of Korea.

The elections took place on 10 May 1948. UNTCOK's supervision was superficial due to a lack of manpower. Amidst widespread corruption and even violence, Rhee and rightist political parties gained a majority in the National Assembly. The National Assembly chose Rhee to be president and he formed a government that claimed to represent all of Korea. In October 1948, the UN General Assembly recognized the new Republic of Korea (ROK). However, a Soviet veto in the Security Council prevented the ROK from actually joining the UN. In turn, the Soviets proceeded with their own 'elections' in North Korea. On 25 August 1948, a Supreme People's Assembly was supposedly elected. One month later, the North Korean Communists formed the Democratic People's Republic of Korea (DPRK), with Kim as the premier.

Both governments considered themselves to be the legitimate rulers of all Korea. Violent skirmishes and raids wracked the border between North and South Korea. Kim focused on gaining control of South Korea through internal subversion. North Korea had been attempting to subvert South Korea internally since the end of the Second World War. Guerrillas in South Korea received direction and arms supplies from North Korea. Many North Korean leaders had originally been Communist leaders in the South. Civil disorder spread to coastal and mountainous regions of South Korea.

The guerrilla war in South Korea came to a head in April 1948 when a major rebellion exploded on Cheju-do, an island off the southern coast. The island was disaffected from the rest of South Korea by its clannish social structure and radical political leanings. In short order, the rebellion spread to Taegu on the mainland. Police sent to suppress the rebellion themselves rebelled around Yosu in October 1948. Rhee instituted harsh measures to suppress the Cheju Rebellion and subversion throughout South Korea, including purging his police force. By the time fighting finally ended after January 1949, 30,000 people had died. In March 1950, North Korea sent thousands of insurgents south to resuscitate the guerrilla war. However, the ROK army was now very efficient at counterinsurgency. Five regiments and 10,000 national police quashed the renewed insurgency.

China

The People's Republic of China also had an interest in events in Korea. American power in the Pacific threatened the PRC. Impressive American air and naval forces and a string of bases in the western Pacific were poised off China's coast. Furthermore, the Chinese Nationalists had received American military assistance throughout the Chinese Civil War. After the civil war, the USA did not recognize the PRC and used its veto power to prevent the PRC from taking the seat designated for China in the UN Security Council. In April 1950, the USA embargoed nearly all goods into China. Mao Zedong, the Chinese leader, was also concerned about maintaining the momentum of the Communist revolution. For Communism in China to develop further, he believed it was necessary to make a firm break with the USA and its imperialist ideology.

In spite of their ideology, the Chinese Communists did not have close ties with the Soviet Union during the Chinese Civil War. Stalin was not forthcoming with military assistance or political support. He had even signed a treaty with the Nationalists. In early 1949, with the civil war drawing to a close, Mao outlined future PRC foreign policy. It was based on the principles of making a fresh start, consolidating the Chinese Communist Party's (CCP) domestic position, fostering economic growth, and 'leaning to one side.' The last phrase meant that, in the context of the superpower competition of the Cold War, the PRC would build ties with the Soviet Union. Mao officially declared that China would 'lean to one side' and establish a special relationship with the Soviet Union on 30 June 1949. This alignment was due partly to shared Communist ideology, but also to increasing confrontation with the USA.

Following Mao's 'lean to one side' statement, the PRC and the Soviet Union became much closer. In August 1949, the Soviet Union sent experts to China to advise in economic reconstruction and military expansion. Stalin offered the PRC $300 million in loans. In early 1950, Mao sought an alliance with the Soviet Union. Consequently, the Sino-Soviet Treaty of Friendship, Alliance, and Mutual Assistance was signed on 14 February 1950. The treaty obliged each country to aid the other in the event of an attack by a third party. China also received another loan of $300 million, which was to be spent on purchasing arms from the Soviet Union.

The Communists strike

When the revolutionary movement in South Korea began to falter, Kim turned to more overt means of unifying the peninsula. In March and April 1949, he visited the Soviet Union and signed an economic and cultural agreement. The two countries also signed an arms pact in March 1949, in which the Soviet Union promised to expand the North Korean armed forces. While in Moscow, Kim pressed Stalin to support a North Korean invasion of South Korea. Stalin would not agree. He did not want to take any actions that might provoke the USA or South Korea into a war. Throughout 1949, Kim lobbied Stalin to back military action.

By September 1949, Stalin and the Soviet Politburo were beginning to consider the merits of military action. Stalin did so for four reasons. First, the victory of the Chinese Communists in the Chinese Civil War increased the strength of the Communist bloc in east Asia. Second, the Soviet Union successfully detonated its first atomic bomb in September, eliminating a major handicap in a war with the USA. Third, the establishment of NATO and worsening relations with the West reduced the prospects of attaining Soviet foreign policy goals through diplomacy. Fourth, there was a perceived weakening of Washington's resolve to fight a war over Korea.

Two events occurred in 1950 that signalled to the Communists that the USA would not fight over Korea. First, on 12 January 1950, Secretary of State Dean Acheson made his infamous speech before the National Press Club in which he implied that South Korea was not an American interest. He stated that the USA was forming a defensive perimeter in the Pacific from the Aleutians to Japan to the Ryukyus and the Philippines. South Korea was not listed within the defensive perimeter. Given the lack of military support already

shown for South Korea, the speech seemed to confirm that the USA would stand aside if the Communists invaded. Second, on 19 January, the House of Representatives narrowly rejected the administration's Korean Aid Bill. Although the vote was reversed in February, the rejection enforced the impression that Americans did not greatly care about Korea.

While the USA waffled over committing to Korea, its policy was solidifying against the Soviet Union. A joint State–Defense Department group completed NSC 68 on 14 April 1950. This document was a reaction to perceived Soviet expansionism. It simplistically viewed international relations as a confrontation between Communism, representing slavery, and the West, representing freedom. It surmised that within four to five years the Soviet Union would be able to attack the USA with nuclear weapons and win a world war. Therefore, American military spending needed to be drastically increased in order to confront Communism not just in Europe but everywhere in the world. Truman supported the document's suggestions. However, many policymakers were sceptical that high military expenditures were necessary or good for the economy. For the next months, NSC 68 sat awaiting approval and implementation.

Stalin entertained three reasons to back a North Korean invasion of South Korea. First, capturing South Korea would increase Soviet security in east Asia. In particular, he wanted to bolster the Soviet position before Japan re-emerged as a major economic and military power. Second, Stalin worried that Rhee might soon attack North Korea. This could create an uncontrollable situation in which the Soviet Union would be forced to intervene. Third, he believed that a war would tie the PRC more firmly to the Soviet Union. A war over Korea would make Chinese rapprochement with the USA nearly impossible.

Kim secretly visited the Soviet Union in April 1950. Here, Stalin finally permitted a North Korean invasion of South Korea. He asked only that Kim assure him that a decisive victory could be achieved and that escalation was impossible. Stalin also emphasized that there would be no direct Soviet intervention. He felt the Soviet Union itself was not yet ready for a military conflict with the West. However, all requested war material would be delivered. Kim then visited Mao in Beijing. Mao agreed that only military action would unify Korea. He doubted that the USA would concern itself over a war in Korea. Kim was also confident and told Mao that his army would capture all of Korea in two to three weeks, long before American intervention would be possible.

On 25 June 1950, North Korea invaded South Korea. North Korean propaganda claimed that the offensive was in reaction to a South Korean attack. The invasion took the ROK and the USA completely by surprise. Truman was outraged. When he disembarked from his airplane in Washington, having flown from Missouri, he was rumoured to have uttered: 'By God, I'm going to let them have it.' For Truman, the invasion was a clear indication of Communists' willingness to use overt aggression to support the expansion of their influence. Both Truman and Acheson believed that Korea was a test of the West's commitment to stand up to Communist aggression. Not fighting would repeat the mistakes of the appeasement of the 1930s and inspire the Communists to conduct further acts of aggression throughout the world.

Despite the previous equivocation, the North Korean invasion was viewed as a clear-cut threat to American interests. If South Korea were conquered, Communist governments would control the entire east Asian mainland (minus Hong Kong) north of Indochina and Communist insurgencies were well underway in Malaya and French Indo-China. This would be a tremendous boon to the Soviet Union. The security of Japan was of particular concern to decision-makers in

Washington. American leaders were determined to keep Soviet influence out of Japan. In fact, the peace treaty with Japan was being delayed in order to prevent the Soviet Union from participating in negotiations over the fate of the country. The victory of the Communists in the Chinese Civil War had already worried American leaders, especially MacArthur, about the safety of Japan. Now the North Korean invasion seemed to threaten this vital interest imminently.

Acheson and Truman immediately brought the issue before the UN Security Council. The Soviet Union had been boycotting the Security Council since January 1950. It was protesting the representation of the Chinese Nationalist government in Taiwan, instead of the PRC, as one of the five permanent members of the Security Council. Without a Soviet delegation to obstruct deliberations, the Security Council quickly adopted a resolution that deplored the North Korean invasion. It urged a cessation of hostilities and the withdrawal of North Korean forces to the 38th Parallel. A second resolution two days later recognized the necessity of urgent military measures and recommended that member states assist South Korea to repel the attack and restore peace. Although Truman and Acheson supported the ideal of collective security, they used the UN mainly as a vehicle for achieving American interests. Securing international peace was a secondary goal.

Truman, Acheson, Louis Johnson (Secretary of Defense), and the JCS met for dinner on 25 June to devise an immediate reaction to the crisis. The capable and level-headed General Omar Bradley, of Second World War fame, chaired the JCS. Three recommendations were discussed: first, to use air power against the North Korean forces; second, to deploy the US Seventh Fleet to protect Taiwan, which might also become threatened soon; and third, to send American military forces directly to South Korea. Johnson and the JCS opposed this last recommendation. They only supported air and naval action. Dispatching ground forces to Korea would weaken the USA's global military position.

Consequently, on 29 June, MacArthur received instructions to use his naval and air forces to defend the ROK. The US Seventh Fleet was placed under his command and he was to ensure that Taiwan was safe against attack. In order to reduce the risk of the conflict escalating into a wider war, operations were to stay clear of the borders of the Soviet Union and China. MacArthur travelled to South Korea on 30 June and observed the military situation. He concluded that only the introduction of American ground forces could save the ROK. MacArthur requested that two divisions be sent to Korea. The JCS, now more confident that the attack was not a prelude to a major battle in Western Europe, approved of the move.

A third resolution was passed in the UN Security Council on 7 July. It recommended the establishment of a United Nations Command to defend South Korea, under the authority of the USA. MacArthur was duly appointed its commander. Fifteen states would eventually contribute troops to the UNC. Britain, New Zealand, Netherlands, France, Canada, Australia, Thailand, and Turkey were the first to offer military assistance. Taiwan's offer of ground forces was declined due to the deleterious effect that such a move would have on relations with the Communists. However, American and ROK forces always far outnumbered the total contribution of all other states.

The Korean War had now begun as the first open war between the USA and a proxy of the Soviet Union. For the two Koreas, their political identity and the very survival of their peoples were at stake. But for the superpowers, influence within east Asia was at issue. Korea was a regional battleground for their global competition.

Avoiding a third world war

The war of maneuver

From July to September 1950, South Korea was on the brink of falling to the North Koreans. Only brilliant and aggressive action by the USA averted this possibility. Both the North Koreans and the Americans utilized highly effective and aggressive operational doctrines that had been refined during the Second World War. However, rather than decisively end the war, these doctrines prolonged it.

For the most part, the North Korean armed forces had been trained and equipped by the Soviet Union. Large numbers of tanks, artillery, aircraft, and small arms had been invested into the North Korean armed forces in 1949 and early 1950. The North Korean People's Army (NKPA) comprised ten

infantry divisions plus an armored brigade, for a total of 130,000 men plus 100,000 trained reserves. Five of the infantry divisions were very well trained and contained troops with combat experience in the Chinese Communist People's Liberation Army (PLA). In the late 1940s, Kim had sent tens of thousands of Koreans to assist the Chinese Communists fighting against the Nationalists in the Chinese Civil War. The PLA released soldiers of Korean nationality, together with their equipment, to join the NKPA in 1949 and 1950. In fact, two PLA divisions directly entered the NKPA, changing in name only. The key formation in the NKPA, though, was the well-trained 105th North Korean Armored Brigade. It was equipped with 120 Soviet T-34 tanks, which

were armed with 85mm guns. North Korea also possessed an air force of 180 Soviet-built Yak fighters and Ilyushin bombers.

Soviet operations advisers devised the invasion plan. It embodied a blitzkrieg assault across the 38th Parallel. Two major armored thrusts were aimed on converging paths towards Seoul. The western thrust, the 1st and 6th North Korean Divisions (a former PLA division) and a detachment from the 105th North Korean Armored Brigade, would strike through Kaesong. The eastern thrust, the 3rd and 4th North Korean Divisions and the rest of the 105th North Korean Armored Brigade, would attack through Uijongbu, the traditional invasion route. In central Korea, the 2nd and 7th North Korean Divisions would mount a secondary assault on Chunchon. Additionally, independent regiments were to advance down the east and west coasts. Division-level planning and reconnaissance were carried out with the help of Soviet advisors. The North Koreans spotted targets for the artillery barrage and probed South

Korean positions for weak spots. North Korean soldiers even mingled with civilians in order to infiltrate South Korean lines. General Kim Ch'aek, a veteran partisan of the Chinese Civil War, commanded the North Korean forces.

The ROK army was not nearly as well trained or equipped as its North Korean counterpart. It numbered 100,000 men in eight weak infantry divisions. Most of these divisions contained only six of their requisite nine infantry battalions. There were only three artillery battalions in the entire army. The South Korean infantry was woefully undertrained: only a handful had seen combat against Communist guerrillas. The ROK lacked both an air force and anti-aircraft batteries to counter North Korean air support. The only American troops in South

Supplied by the Soviet Union, the T-34 tanks of the 105th North Korean Armored Brigade spearheaded the invasion of South Korea. The South Koreans and Americans initially had no defense against the T-34's heavy armor and high-powered 85mm gun. (The Tank Museum, Bovington)

South Korean soldiers marching to battle in July 1950.
The ROK army was extremely unprepared for war in
1950. Many of the men had no military training and little
proper equipment. (US Army)

Korea were the 500 men of the Korean
Military Advisory Group (KMAG).

South and North Korea were more evenly
matched on the sea. The North Korean navy
was composed of approximately 50 small
vessels; a mix of patrol boats, minesweepers,
torpedo boats, and one escort. South Korea
had 39 small craft, primarily patrol boats and
minesweepers. By neglecting seapower, Kim
abandoned virtually any capability to interfere
with possible UK and US naval operations.
These two naval powers would easily be able
to reinforce South Korea and mount strikes
anywhere along the Korean littoral.

The terrain of Korea is not optimal for a
blitzkrieg. Only about 150 miles (240km) wide,
the peninsula is suited for a strong in-depth
defense. Most of the country is comprised of
rugged hills with steep slopes, intersected by
valleys. The roads primarily run through these
valleys. The Taebaek mountain range runs
north to south through the entire eastern half
of the peninsula. Even in the flatter western
half, narrow valleys, rice paddies, and jagged
hills make mobile warfare difficult. Climatic
conditions are no more conducive to military

operations. The summers are very hot and
humid. The winters, on the other hand, are
extremely cold, with near-Arctic conditions.
The Yellow Sea often freezes. In the spring,
melting snow creates large floods and
mudslides, which restrict movement.

Nevertheless, the dispositions of the ROK
army made a blitzkrieg entirely viable.
Major-General Chae Pyongdok, a veteran of
the Japanese army, commanded the ROK
armed forces. He wanted to contain any
North Korean attack at the 38th Parallel and
rejected a planned withdrawal to stronger
positions, such as behind the Han river. The
38th Parallel was on comparatively flat
ground, lacking ridges or river-lines on which
to form a defensive. Chae strung out four
divisions and one regiment along the parallel.

On 25 June, at 4.40 am, the North Koreans
attacked. Soviet advisors guided the initial
breakthrough. The general pattern of the
attack was as follows. First heavy artillery
bombarded the attack zones. Next the infantry
and tanks moved forward, smashing the
bewildered South Korean defenders. Finally
the mechanized North Korean units pressed
on to their objectives, cutting South Korean
supply lines and pursuing defeated units.

The 1st ROK Division defended the
approach to Seoul via Kaesong, known as the
'western corridor.' Colonel Paik Sun Yup

A North Korean command group. Soviet advisors guided the initial breakthrough. Thereafter, the North Koreans controlled operations. But without the Soviets' experience, North Korean officers were less able to conduct combined-arms operations. (US Army)

river. Artillery fire supported counterattacks and was directed against North Korean penetrations. Nevertheless, unable to counter the North Korean tanks, Paik was pushed back. He wrote in his memoirs that many soldiers acquired 'T-34 disease' and panicked at the sight of tanks. Some of Paik's men resorted to Japanese suicide tactics. Laden with high explosives, they threw themselves upon oncoming tanks.

The 6th ROK Division, under the able Kim Chong O, also fought well and managed to halt the 2nd and 7th North Korean Divisions for three days before Chunchon. Elsewhere, however, the front was crumbling. In particular, the undermanned 7th and 2nd ROK Divisions on Paik's right flank disintegrated against the North Korean

commanded the division. At only 29 years of age, he was the youngest divisional commander in the ROK army. On 25 June, the veteran 6th North Korean Division overwhelmed Paik's forward regiment and captured Kaesong, the ancient capital of Korea, in four hours. Paik put up a fierce fight with his remaining two regiments. Commanding from the front, he withdrew to a pre-arranged defensive line on the Imjin

Paik Sun Yup stands third from the far left with this group of senior officials, including Matthew Ridgway (second from far right), for a photo in 1951. In 1950, Paik was the 29-year-old commander of the 1st ROK Division. Generally considered to be the best South Korean field officer in the war, Paik would command the ROK armed forces by the end of the war. (US Air Force)

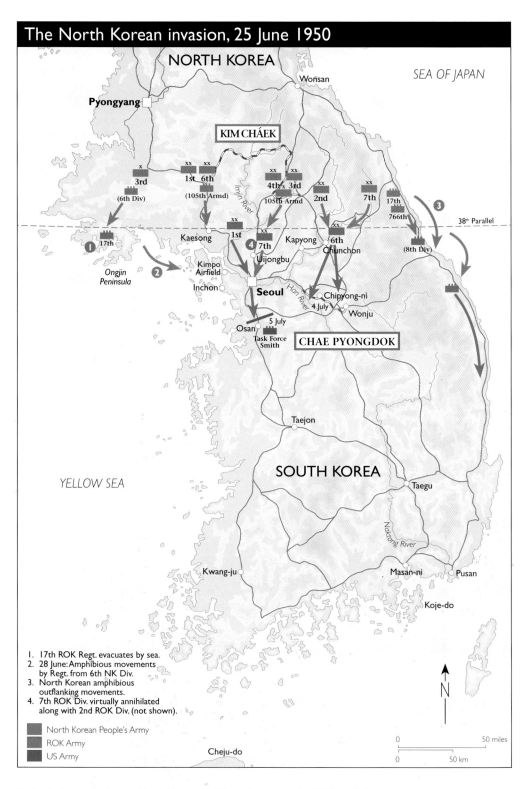

The North Korean invasion, 25 June 1950

NORTH KOREA

SEA OF JAPAN

Wonsan

Pyongyang

KIM CHÁEK

x 3rd
(6th Div)

xx xx
1st 6th
(105th Armd)

xx xx
4th 3rd
105th Armd

xx
2nd

xx
7th

xx
17th
766th

38th Parallel

Imjin River

17th
Ongjin Peninsula

Kaesong

xx
1st

xx
7th
Uijongbu

Kapyong

xx
6th
Chunchon

(8th Div)

Kimpo Airfield
Inchon

Seoul

Han River

Chipyong-ni
4 July

Wonju

Osan 5 July
Task Force Smith

CHAE PYONGDOK

Taejon

YELLOW SEA

SOUTH KOREA

Taegu

Naktong River

Kwang-ju

Masan-ni

Pusan

Koje-do

1. 17th ROK Regt. evacuates by sea.
2. 28 June: Amphibious movements by Regt. from 6th NK Div.
3. North Korean amphibious outflanking movements.
4. 7th ROK Div. virtually annihilated along with 2nd ROK Div. (not shown).

North Korean People's Army
ROK Army
US Army

N

0   50 miles
0   50 km

Cheju-do

Under Soviet supervision, the North Koreans rapidly broke through the ROK army's lines in a blitzkrieg assault on South Korea on 25 June 1950.

armored column advancing towards Uijongbu. In the ROK military headquarters in Seoul, there was disorder. With communications disrupted, Chae had no idea of the situation at the front. By the end of 26 June, the North Koreans had invested Uijongbu and looked upon an open road to Seoul. Consequently, Paik sought to withdraw across the Han, but Chae ordered him to 'Fight to the death in your present positions.' The roads and trains out of Seoul were clogged with people trying to flee. In the confusion, the sole bridge across the Han was prematurely blown up. Hundreds of civilians were crossing the bridge at that moment. Forty-four thousand soldiers and most of the army's heavy equipment were now cut off to the north. Although in a disorganized state, Paik managed to pull his division across the Han near the western outskirts of Seoul. Thus, by 28 June, the ROK army had been completely routed and Seoul had fallen.

Major-General Chung Il Kwon, Chae's successor, decided to withdraw and preserve the ROK army rather than engage in further last-ditch defensives. Major-General Kim Hong Il took charge of delaying actions as the ROK army withdrew to the Naktong river. Kim

Hong Il had been a senior officer with the Chinese Nationalists in the Second World War and had experience of commanding large formations. His steady efforts provided the time needed for the build-up of American forces in Korea and the construction of the Pusan Perimeter (see page 24).

Upon the outbreak of war, the US and British navies quickly deployed to the waters surrounding Korea. Because the US Seventh Fleet was dispatched to the Taiwan Straits, the initial US navy commitment to Korea consisted of only one fleet carrier (USS *Valley Forge*), one heavy cruiser, and eight destroyers, known as Task Force 77. Eventually, the bulk of the Seventh Fleet deployed off Korea. On 27 June, the British government decided to place ships of the Royal Navy Far East Fleet, which included a light fleet carrier (HMS *Triumph*) at the disposal of Vice-Admiral C. Turner Joy, the commander of American naval forces in the Far East. The fleets blockaded North Korea,

A group of South Korean soldiers in a rice paddy wait to advance on 6 September 1950. Despite their initial rout, the ROK army survived the opening North Korean onslaught and continued fighting throughout the war. South Korea provided over half of the UNC's manpower. (US Army)

and naval aircraft from both carriers launched strikes against enemy targets. Meanwhile, the US Far East Air Force quickly swept the skies of North Korean aircraft.

After the decision to commit ground forces, the USA hurriedly ferried formations into South Korea. The Eighth US Army was sent to Korea, commanded by General Walton Walker. Rhee placed the ROK army under UNC command. The first reinforcements, the 24th and 25th US Infantry Divisions, arrived directly from Japan. Their men had been enjoying the comforts of occupational life in Japan and were not ready for combat. Like the ROK army, the two divisions were not equipped to combat T-34s. On 5 July, a detachment of the 24th US Division, known as Task Force Smith, was assigned to defend Osan. North Korean armor pressed the Americans back to Taejon, an important road hub, within a week. There, the entire division, attempting to make a stand, was overrun. Its commander, Major-General William Dean, was personally involved in the front-line combat and was captured in the ensuing rout. One North Korean officer, Lieutenant Oak Hyung-uk, later told historian John Toland that many Americans were too frightened to fight.

As ROK and American formations fought delaying actions, Walker established the Pusan Perimeter, a defensive line which ran north along the Naktong river and then east to the west. Pusan was a vital port on the southern tip of the peninsula through which most American forces arrived. The first threat came from the 6th North Korean Division. These veterans of the Chinese Civil War had made a rapid, if circuitous, advance through south-western Korea and were now threatening to outflank Walker's line in the south. The 25th US Division barely stopped them less than 30 miles (48km) from Pusan. Kim Ch'aek tried to exploit this breach in the First Battle of the Naktong Bulge. His headquarters hoped to pre-empt further American reinforcements. But by 24 August, the attacks here and at Taegu had been thrown back with heavy casualties.

Reinforcements were now arriving daily. Better American bazookas and heavy M-26 Pershing tanks had arrived that could counter the T-34s. The North Koreans waited until 3 September to make their major assault in the Second Battle of the Naktong Bulge. However, by then North Korean strength was ebbing. With only 98,000 men, they faced 180,000 UNC soldiers. Walker used his superior firepower and reserves effectively and threw back the attackers. Exact North Korean casualties from the beginning of the war to this point are unknown, but some American estimates place them as high as 60,000. The ROK army and the American forces suffered 70,000 and 16,000 casualties respectively.

While Walker halted the North Koreans around the Pusan Perimeter, MacArthur was planning a more decisive action to the north. MacArthur is one of the great figures of the Korean War. At the beginning of the war, his reputation was gigantic from his victories in the Pacific War. After 1945, he had governed the occupation and reconstruction of Japan. So great was his influence that Washington made few attempts to control his actions. MacArthur was a devout exponent of decisive warfare. Throughout the Pacific War, he had engaged in a series of amphibious assaults to outflank the Japanese, get behind their supply lines, and bypass their strongpoints. Thus, in Korea he did not want to continue a frontal battle at Pusan, but sought to annihilate the North Koreans in one swift stroke.

MacArthur proposed an amphibious landing at Inchon, the port for Seoul. A landing there offered the opportunity to sever North Korea's lines of communication and trap its army to the south. Inchon was an extremely dangerous and risky point to attack. City-fighting is costly under the best of circumstances; it is even more so when soldiers must first disembark from assault craft directly under defending fire. Additionally, the Inchon harbor had deep tidal shifts, high sea walls, a narrow channel, broad mudflats, and fortified islands. The tide fell 20 feet (6m) twice per day. MacArthur, though, believed that these factors actually made Inchon an attractive

Marines climb from their landing craft to assault Inchon on 15 September 1950. Inchon harbor had large tidal shifts, mudflats, a narrow channel, fortified islands, and a high seawall. In this photo, Marines are using ladders to ascend part of the seawall. (The Historical Branch, United States Marine Corps)

point to attack. The North Koreans would never expect it. The JCS initially were sceptical about the attack. But MacArthur won them over through skilfully presenting his case to the Chief of the Army, General Lawton Collins, and the Chief of Naval Operations, Admiral Forrest Sherman, at a strategic planning conference in Tokyo.

The 1st US Marine and 7th US Infantry Divisions would mount the assault as part of the newly formed X US Corps. Lieutenant-General Edward Almond, MacArthur's chief of staff, was given command of the corps. Circumventing Walker, Almond answered directly to MacArthur. The X US Corps represented the last of MacArthur's reserves. If his gamble failed and disaster struck at Inchon, there would be no troops left to retake South Korea.

The troops were to be put ashore on 15 September in tidal 'windows' – the period when the tide was high enough for landing craft to reach the shore. First, the

Marines would seize Wolmi-do, the island controlling the harbor. Then, they would press into the city and on to capture Kimpo Airfield. Next, Seoul, the most important rail and road hub in South Korea, would be assaulted. Finally, both divisions would block the enemy retreat from the Pusan Perimeter. Ironically, Kim Il Sung and Kim Ch'aek were aware of the likelihood of an American amphibious attack at Inchon. However, they decided to stake everything on the Second Battle of the Naktong Bulge and left Inchon relatively undefended.

Early on 15 September, UNC naval and air forces bombarded Wolmi-do. MacArthur was personally present aboard the flagship of the amphibious assault force, the USS *Mount McKinley*. At 6.33 am, the first battalion of the 5th Marine Regiment landed and took the key point on the island without a single fatality. The remaining battalions of the regiment assaulted Inchon itself at the next tidal window at 5.30 pm. The disembarking Marines clambered over the sea wall and through enemy bunkers to capture the dominating ground surrounding the beachhead. Meanwhile, the 1st Marine Regiment landed on the city's southern outskirts. By morning the Marines had

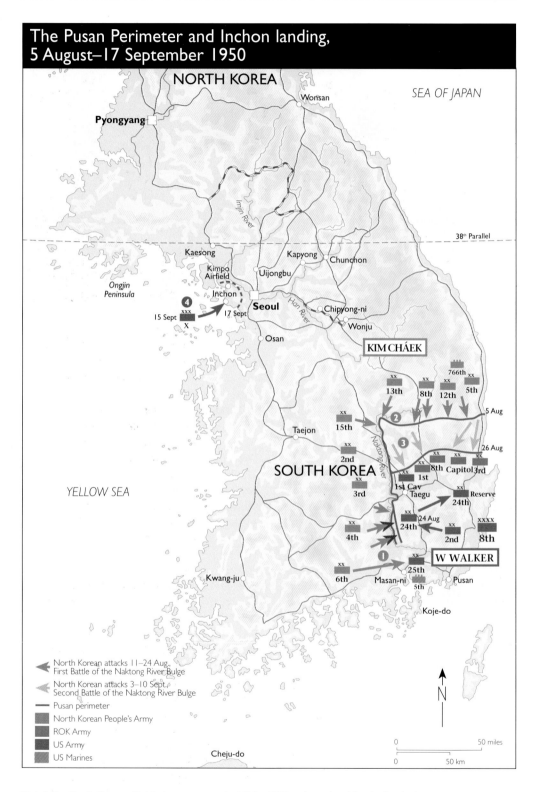

The Pusan Perimeter and Inchon landing, 5 August–17 September 1950

NORTH KOREA

SEA OF JAPAN

Pyongyang

Wonsan

Imjin River

38th Parallel

Kaesong

Kapyong   Chunchon

Kimpo
Airfield   Uijongbu

*Ongjin
Peninsula*   Inchon

15 Sept   17 Sept   **Seoul**

XXX   X   Han River   Chipyong-ni

Osan   Wonju

KIM CHÁEK

766th
XX   XX   XX   XX
13th   8th   12th   5th

5 Aug

Taejon   XX
15th

Naktong River

2   26 Aug

XX   XX   XX
2nd

3   XX   XX   XX
XX   8th Capitol 3rd
1st

SOUTH KOREA

XX   XX
3rd   1st Cav
Taegu   XX   Reserve
24th

YELLOW SEA

XX   24 Aug
24th

XX   XX   XXXX
4th   24th   2nd   **8th**

1   XX   **W WALKER**

Kwang-ju   XX
6th   Masan-ni   Pusan
5th

Koje-do

North Korean attacks 11–24 Aug.,
First Battle of the Naktong River Bulge

North Korean attacks 3–10 Sept.,
Second Battle of the Naktong River Bulge

Pusan perimeter

North Korean People's Army

ROK Army

US Army   Cheju-do

US Marines

N

0 _____ 50 miles
0 _____ 50 km

To halt the North Koreans, Eighth Army commander Walton Walker formed a defensive line in the southeast corner of Korea, known as the Pusan Perimeter, in August 1950.

A dramatic picture of Marines engaged in street fighting during the battle for Seoul. American incendiary bombs, artillery shells, and tanks reduced the city to rubble. (US Army)

pressed 6 miles (10km) inland and controlled the Inchon–Seoul supply route.

The North Koreans, facing the X US Corps, retreated to Seoul where 20,000 held out in a last-ditch stand. Major-General O. P. Smith, commander of the Marine Division, planned a two-pronged attack to take Seoul from the north and southwest. Kimpo fell to the northern group on 18 September. Anxious to capture Seoul, Almond threw the 7th US Division's 32nd Regiment into the attack from the southeast. The fight for Seoul was ferocious. UNC artillery fire and close air

OPPOSITE
1. On 11 August, the 6th North Korean Division tried to outflank the Eighth Army line in the south, initiating the First Battle of the Naktong River Bulge.
2. The bulk of the North Korean forces attacked the apex of the Eighth Army line.
3. Unsuccessful in the first battle, the North Koreans made a carefully prepared attempt to break the Pusan Perimeter in the Second Battle of the Naktong Bulge (3–10 September), but again the Eighth Army held fast.
4. Meanwhile, MacArthur landed the X US Corps at Inchon on 15 September, threatening the North Korean supply lines. This caused the collapse of the entire North Korean People's Army in the following week.

support struck the city heavily. Napalm caused incendiary fires. Many civilians died in the fighting. The North Koreans fought fanatically, using suicide squads to destroy American tanks. They were finally defeated by 27 September when the American and UN flags were raised over the capitol.

Walker broke out from the Pusan Perimeter on 23 September. Three days later, the 1st US Cavalry and 7th US Divisions linked at Osan, trapping large numbers of Koreans. The NKPA fell into a rout. Trapped, the North Korean forces west of Osan were smashed. Those to the east collapsed as they retreated north. Many soldiers took refuge in the Taebaeks as guerrillas. Ranking officers frequently surrendered to the American and ROK forces. The battered 13th North Korean Division's chief of staff even shot its commanding general – who wanted to continue reckless assaults – in order to allow the men to retreat. By the time they were back across the 38th Parallel, the North Koreans had lost over 150,000 men. The UNC captured 125,000 prisoners. UNC losses in the offensive, including Inchon, were 18,000.

Inchon was a stunning and brilliant victory for the UNC. The threat to South Korea was completely overturned and the NKPA virtually annihilated. However, while MacArthur's maneuver warfare was outstandingly effective in annihilating the North Koreans, it did not create a stable basis for peace. Rather, the decisiveness of the victory greatly threatened the Soviet Union and the PRC.

The Chinese enter the war

American entry into the Korean War greatly concerned the Chinese Communists. An American victory in Korea would threaten their security and ideological interests. Indeed, Mao and Premier Zhou Enlai viewed the American intervention as part of a grand plan to control east Asia. Accordingly, on 13 July 1950, four armies were dispatched to the Korean border to form the Northeast Border Defense Army (NBDA). It would defend China's border and support the operations of the North Korean armed forces. Historian Chen Jian describes in *China's Road to the Korean War* how, at a meeting of the Chinese Politburo on 4 August 1950, Mao said: 'If the US imperialists won the war they would become more arrogant and would threaten us. We should not fail to assist the Koreans. We must lend them our hands in the form of sending our military volunteers there.' However, Mao could not yet intervene because of the unpreparedness of the PLA.

The Inchon landing brought the question of Chinese intervention to a head. As the NKPA disintegrated, first Pak Il-yu, North Korean Minister of Interior Affairs, and then Kim himself requested immediate Chinese intervention to save North Korea. For Mao and the CCP, the annihilation of the NKPA increased the threat that the USA posed to China. The battle line was rapidly approaching Manchuria, a vital industrial region. On 24 September, Zhou protested the accidental American bombing of Andong to the UN. Two days later, Nie Rongzhen, the acting PLA chief of staff, told K. M. Panikkar, Indian ambassador to the PRC, that the PRC would not passively await an American advance to the Sino-Korean border.

The American landing at Inchon also shocked Stalin. If the USA occupied all of

Korea, the entire balance of power in east Asia would be upset. American forces would be directly on Soviet borders as well as China's. Nevertheless, Stalin was still unwilling to risk a direct military confrontation. Therefore, Stalin asked Mao if China was in a position to intervene. He promised military equipment and that the Soviet air force would provide air superiority over the Chinese armies.

Mao did not respond to Kim and Stalin's requests until 2 October. At a specially convened meeting of the CCP Politburo, Mao announced his intention to intervene. After the meeting, with the Politburo's tentative support, Mao sent a telegram to Stalin, comprehensively summarizing his plans. A portion of the PLA would be sent to Korea as the Chinese People's Volunteers (CPV). Although he expected American retaliation against Chinese soil, Mao's goal was nothing less than the decisive annihilation of the UNC forces in Korea. He hoped to avoid a stalemate, which would drain China's resources and stunt its economic reconstruction.

Zhou was sent to Moscow to ask for large amounts of aid and weapons, as well as reconfirmation of Soviet air support. Before his departure, at midnight on 2 October, Zhou told Panikkar that if the USA crossed the 38th Parallel, the PRC would 'not sit still and do nothing.' Nevertheless, in all likelihood, there was little the USA could have done to dissuade Mao from intervening at this point. Zhou's message was probably just meant to buy time for the CPV to concentrate in North Korea. On 3 October, Mao appointed Peng Dehuai to command the CPV. Peng was one of the PLA's best leaders and was known for his courage in tough situations. The final orders to the CPV to enter Korea were issued on 8 October.

The Chinese decision to intervene gave Stalin what he wanted. When he met with Zhou on 11 October, Stalin said that the Soviet Union would provide all of the artillery, armor, aircraft, and military equipment required, but that the PRC would have to pay for it. Mao tried unsuccessfully to bargain with Stalin. Given the threat that the USA posed, though, he had no choice but to continue with intervention.

Meanwhile, the Eighth Army approached the 38th Parallel. MacArthur was hypnotized by the allure of total victory and disregarded the repeated Chinese warnings. Nor did many in the American government take the warnings seriously. MacArthur and the American government sought to unify Korea under the ROK. In late September, the JCS and Acheson decided to pursue the NKPA north of the parallel as long as there was no threat of major Soviet or Chinese intervention. Secretary of Defense George C. Marshall even told MacArthur that the government wanted him to 'feel unhampered tactically and strategically to proceed north of the 38th parallel.' On 1 October, ROK troops crossed the 38th Parallel, followed by the rest of the Eighth Army on 7 October. Despite the increasing momentum to unify Korea, Truman was concerned about the repercussions of crossing the 38th Parallel. He arranged a meeting with MacArthur on Wake Island to discuss the situation. At the hugely publicized meeting on 15 October, MacArthur reassured Truman that there were no signs of Chinese or Soviet intent to intervene.

A UN resolution in the General Assembly on 7 October permitted the UNC to advance across the 38th Parallel and unify Korea. The Soviet Union had returned to the Security Council in August. To overcome its veto, the USA pushed through a special procedure in November 1950, known as 'Uniting for Peace.' It stipulated that, if a veto paralyzed the Security Council in an emergency, the General Assembly could rule on the concerned matter as long as a two-thirds majority pertained.

Back in Korea, MacArthur deployed his corps on diverging lines of advance. The Eighth Army advanced in the west, taking Pyongyang on 20 October and then moving on toward the Yalu. The X US Corps, still acting directly under MacArthur, conducted a belated amphibious landing at Wonsan on 26 October (which the I ROK Corps had already beaten them to), and drove north. UNC front-line strength was approximately 200,000 men.

A column of Chinese infantry crossing the Yalu river into Korea. In October and November 1950, the People's Liberation Army, under the pseudonym of the Chinese People's Volunteers, massed in the northern reaches of Korea, waiting to spring their trap against the carelessly advancing UNC forces. (Chinese News Agency)

The CPV, unlike the NKPA, was poorly equipped. It lacked artillery and was not mechanized. Despite the recent increase in Soviet assistance, most of its small arms and ammunition had been captured from the Nationalist Chinese or the Japanese. Logistics were primarily organized through civilian laborers who carried supplies to the front on foot. Thus, the CPV could not advance far without suffering supply difficulties. However, tremendous manpower and a strong base of recent combat experience offset these disadvantages. Most CPV soldiers had experienced combat in the large field operations at the end of the Chinese Civil War. They were hardy marchers and adept at off-road movement. Peng emphasized the quick and bold movement of infantry to encircle and overwhelm the enemy. Attacks were to be conducted at night when the element of surprise would facilitate a breakthrough. Most Chinese leaders, buoyed by their success in the Second World War and the Chinese Civil War, believed that deception, stealth, and night fighting would enable their poorly armed soldiers to overcome Western technological and materiel superiority.

The CPV was composed of the Thirteenth and Ninth CPV Army Corps, for

OPPOSITE
The Chinese entered the Korean War in force on 25 November 1950. In the west, the Thirteenth CPV Army Corps threatened to encircle the Eighth Army. The 2nd US Division was cut off at Kunu-ri and virtually annihilated struggling south. The entire army was forced south in a disorganized rout. In the east, the Ninth CPV Army Corps encircled the 1st US Marine Division of the X US Corps at the Chosin reservoir.

a total of about 300,000 men. The former, commanded by General Deng Hua, contained four CPV armies, of three divisions each. Deng had carefully trained the Thirteenth CPV Army Corps. Its soldiers were of a very high caliber. For example, the 38th CPV Army of the Thirteenth CPV Army Corps was known as an elite formation from its performance in the Chinese Civil War. The three armies of the Ninth CPV Army Corps, on the other hand, had been preparing for an invasion of Taiwan and were not ready to face the mountainous terrain and freezing winter weather of Korea. The North Korean armed

General Peng Dehuai, seated on the left, commanded the Chinese People's Volunteers. He was a realistic and level-headed commander. Unfortunately, he was executed during the Cultural Revolution after privately questioning Mao's policies. (Xinhua)

The Communist Second Phase Offensive, 25 November 1950

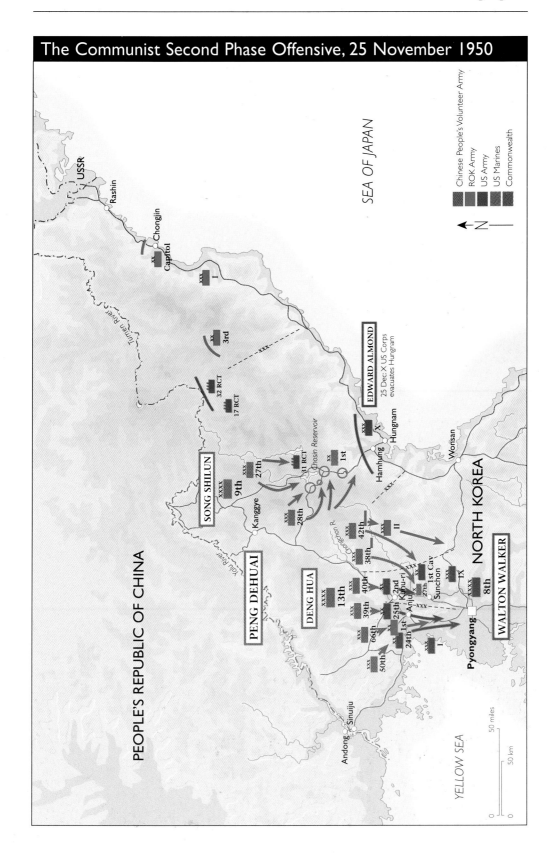

Chinese People's Volunteer Army
ROK Army
US Army
US Marines
Commonwealth

N

SEA OF JAPAN

USSR

Rashin

Chongjin

Capitol
XX

I
XXX

3rd
XX

32 RCT
XXX

17 RCT
XXX

EDWARD ALMOND
25 Dec X US Corps
evacuates Hungnam

SONG SHILUN

9th
XXXX

27th
XXX

31 RCT
XXX

Chosin Reservoir

1st
XX

X
XXX

Hamhung

Hungnam

Wonsan

NORTH KOREA

28th
XXX

Kanggye

PENG DEHUAI

Yalu River

Chongchon R.

42nd
XXX

38th
XXX

II
XXX

DENG HUA

13th
XXXX

40th
XXX

2nd
XX

Kunu-ri

1st Cav
XXX

27th

Sunchon

IX
XXX

WALTON WALKER

8th
XXXX

39th
XXX

25th
XX

1st
XXX

Anju
X

66th
XXX

24th
XXX

I
XXX

Pyongyang

50th
XXX

PEOPLE'S REPUBLIC OF CHINA

Andong

Sinuiju

Tumen River

YELLOW SEA

50 miles

50 km

0

0

forces, although given some autonomy, also fell under Peng's command.

The Thirteenth CPV Army Corps first crossed the Yalu on 14 October 1950. Two weeks later, it mounted a limited attack on the II ROK Corps in order to stunt the Eighth Army advance; this attack was known as the First Phase Offensive. After smashing an ROK and an American regiment, Peng returned to the defensive, waiting for the UNC to advance and overextend itself. Although Walker ordered a tactical withdrawal, MacArthur did not appreciate the gravity of what had occurred. He believed that only a small number of Chinese troops were actually in Korea and that a quick advance would pre-empt further intervention. On 24 November, MacArthur and Walker resumed the UNC advance, falling into Peng's trap. Expecting a quick and painless end to the war, UNC soldiers and officers advanced recklessly. Formations became strung out and did not take proper precautions against a counterattack. Rumour spread that the American troops would be 'home by Christmas.'

On the evening of 25 November, Peng and the CPV sprung upon the renewed UNC advance to open the Second Phase Offensive. The Thirteenth CPV Army Corps, of 180,000 men, was to crush the II ROK Corps

in central Korea and then cut off the retreat of the I and IX US Corps to the west. Mao and Peng hoped this offensive might unify the peninsula under Communist control. The assaulting Chinese infantry moved off-road to encircle and then overwhelm UNC units. Lacking sufficient radios, the Chinese used bugles, drums, and other instruments to coordinate their movements. These surprise attacks were very disorienting to the average UNC soldier. By the end of 26 November, the II ROK Corps had completely disintegrated, and the Chinese were surrounding the 2nd US Infantry Division. Meanwhile, the Chinese pressed the fronts of the two American corps in order to pin them against the flanking movement. The I US Corps was forced to retreat hurriedly down the coast. The entire Eighth Army was threatened with encirclement.

Disregarding reports from the front, Walker and MacArthur would not permit the 2nd US Division to retreat until 28 November. By then, the 38th CPV Army had cut off the division's escape route, the

American infantry under Chinese attack in North Korea in late 1950. American soldiers had been expecting to be shipped home, but instead found themselves in a new, much more difficult, conflict. (US Army Military History Institute)

Chinese infantry advancing at night. The Chinese were adept at infiltration tactics, night combat, and off-road movement. Their surprise attacks, accompanied by eerie whistles and bugles, disconcerted UNC soldiers. (Chinese National Army Museum)

road from Kunu-ri to Sunchon. The Chinese ensconced themselves on the hillsides overlooking the road and maintained a constant rain of small arms fire on to the road-bound 2nd US Division. They used satchel charges, grenades, and mortar shelling to destroy American vehicles and equipment. American troops quickly lost all

cohesion. The road became filled with the wreckage of American tanks, artillery, and transport vehicles. UNC air strikes napalmed the hillsides and hampered the CPV encirclement. The 38th CPV Army was unable physically to block the road, allowing disordered American soldiers to escape.

The Ninth CPV Army Corps marching in North Korea about the time of the battle for the Chosin reservoir. These men had been training for an amphibious landing on Taiwan and were not prepared for the near-Arctic conditions of the Chosin reservoir. Thousands died from the cold. (Xinhua)

By 30 November, the remnants of the 2nd US Division met with the forward positions of the 27th Commonwealth Brigade, which had been attempting to relieve them. The division had taken 5,000 casualties. Meanwhile, the rest of the IX and I US Corps (with some elements of the 2nd US Division) retreated to safety via Anju on the west coast. The Chinese had not moved fast enough to block this escape route.

In the mountains around the Chosin reservoir, the Ninth CPV Army Corps of 120,000 men was preparing to encircle the X US Corps. In accordance with MacArthur's orders for an offensive to the Yalu, the 1st US Marine Division had advanced along the western edge of the Chosin reservoir toward the Yalu. To Almond's ire, Smith had wisely slowed the advance of the Marine Division in order to concentrate his forces and maintain a steady flow of supplies. As the Marines marched north, the temperature dropped below freezing and it began to snow.

The 1st US Marine Division was an elite formation. Many of the Marines had extensive combat experience in the Pacific War. This foundation of combat experience was one of the major reasons that the Marines performed well in Korea. Another was the degree to which the Marines emphasized loyalty and unit cohesion. The Marines were committed to standing together and fighting it out in difficult situations.

On the night of 27 November, the Ninth CPV Army Corps encircled the Marines at the Chosin reservoir. In the ensuing battle, the Marines fought their way out, driving south to Chinhung-ni.

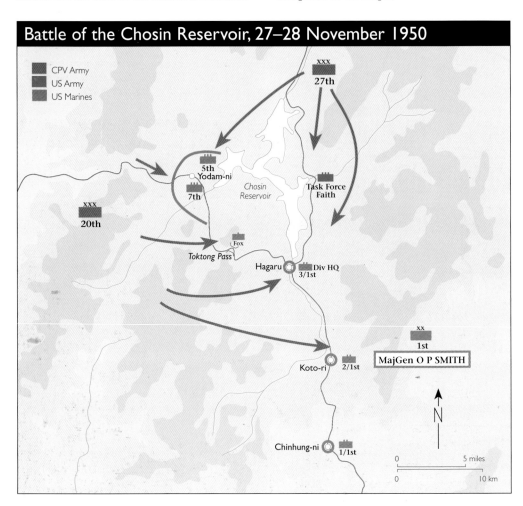

Battle of the Chosin Reservoir, 27–28 November 1950

CPV Army
US Army
US Marines

XXX
27th

XXX
20th

5th
Yodam-ni

7th

Chosin
Reservoir

Task Force
Faith

Fox

Toktong Pass

Hagaru   Div HQ
3/1st

Koto-ri   2/1st

XX
1st

MajGen O P SMITH

N

Chinhung-ni   1/1st

0   5 miles

0   10 km

On the night of 27 November, the Chinese struck. They cut off the lead 5th and 7th Marine Regiments at Yudam-ni and surrounded the 1st Marine Regiment at Hagaru and Koto-ri. In mass numbers, the Chinese mounted frontal assaults on the Marine positions. Corporal Arthur Koch, a squad leader in the 5th Marine Regiment, described the experience of a Chinese attack in Martin Russ's book *Breakout*:

It was enough to make your hair stand on end ... When the bugles died away we heard a voice through a megaphone and then the blast of a police whistle. I was plenty scared, but who wasn't? I couldn't believe my eyes when I saw them in the moonlight. It was like the snow coming to life, and they were shouting and shaking their fists – just raising hell ... The Chinese didn't come at us by fire and maneuver ... they came in a rush like a pack of mad dogs. Even though I was ready it was a terrible shock.

Nearly every man took part in the fighting. All Marines, whatever their specialization, were trained to fight as infantrymen. Sergeant James H. Fearns was a mechanic who quickly departed from his duties to serve as a front-line infantryman. He found the Chinese to be much more determined opponents than the North Koreans. The North Koreans would retreat once pushed off a position. The Chinese, on the other hand, would stand and fight. However, the Chinese often made gross tactical errors. Besides frontally attacking the same strong positions repeatedly, they did not know how to exploit a breakthrough. They would mill around on captured hills, making wonderful targets. Despite being outnumbered, the Marines inflicted hideous casualties on the Chinese frontal assaults. Every time the Chinese captured a ridge, the Marines counterattacked and drove them back off it.

A load of napalm dropped from a Corsair explodes against the Chinese blocking the retreat of the Marines from the Chosin reservoir. In spite of being surrounded, the Marines fought their way out, destroying several CPV divisions in the process. (US Naval Institute)

On 29 November, Smith ordered Colonel Homer Litzenberg, commanding the 7th Marine Regiment at Yudam-ni to break out to Hagaru. One battalion attacked cross-country and broke through the Chinese block at the Toktong Pass, while the bulk of the two regiments pressed down the road frontally. Steep hills and ridges lined both sides of the road. The Chinese were able to fire upon the column and injure Marines, destroy transports, and temporarily block the road. Individual Marines independently remedied problems as they arose, such as clearing wreckage in the road, assisting wounded men, or engaging the Chinese. In the daytime, US Marine Corps Corsair fighter-bombers napalmed, strafed, and bombed the hillsides. Through their combined efforts, the column trudged forward.

On 3 December, the vanguard of the column entered Hagaru. From Hagaru, the entire Marine force pressed on to Koto-ri and then to the X US Corps lines and safety at Chinhung-ni. Smith allegedly told reporters: 'Retreat, hell – we're attacking in another direction.' The entire X US Corps evacuated Hungnam and left North Korea on Christmas Day. The Marines suffered 4,400 battle casualties in the fighting around the Chosin reservoir. The Ninth CPV Army Corps was badly mauled and had to be withdrawn to Manchuria for reorganization. More than 20,000 dead Chinese, most killed by the cold, littered the hillsides, frozen and covered with snow.

However, the Marines' heroism at Chosin cannot mask the catastrophic results of the Chinese intervention for the UNC. The UNC fell back all the way to the 38th Parallel in the longest retreat in American military history, known by the troops at the front as the 'Big Bug-Out.' Even though only 13,000 casualties were suffered, the UNC ground forces, for the most part, were transformed into a disorganized mob. Captain Charles Bussey, of the 77th US Engineer Combat Company, described his recollections of the retreat in his book *Firefight at Yechon*:

We'd been humiliated, debased, overwhelmed – routed … The news writers would slant it all to sound like a minor setback. Take it from me, however, it was carnage. Intelligence said they hit us with one-third of a million men. I believe it. They turned our Army into a leaderless horde, running headlong for Pusan. Our soldiers had lost every bit of confidence in all of their leaders, from the commander in chief down to platoon leaders.

American decision-makers now believed that they were faced with the choice of either withdrawing entirely from Korea – tantamount to surrendering – or escalating the conflict further. Escalation could bring the Soviet Union directly into the fighting. Thus, the conflict in Korea threatened to trigger a Third World War.

The war of attrition

The rout of the Eighth Army placed UNC general headquarters in a state of total panic. MacArthur dispatched a series of frantic reports to Washington warning of the impending annihilation of the UNC. Despite the risk of further escalation, he called for direct military action against China. The use of atomic weapons was not excluded in his demands. Despite MacArthur's reports, escalating the war appeared very dangerous to the Truman administration and the USA's allies. Seeking total victory against North Korea had already brought China into the conflict. Waging total war against China might cause the Soviet Union to intervene as well. With very weak conventional forces in Europe, the West could not risk a war with the Soviet Union. Even if the Soviet Union did not intervene, the USA and UNC would be immersed in a wider war in Asia that would demand a huge military commitment. In the following weeks, although still searching for a course of action, the USA hesitantly supported two resolutions in the UN for an immediate cease-fire. Zhou rejected the resolutions. It was evident that the USA needed to find an alternative between withdrawal and escalation: in other words, a means of fighting a limited war.

In a limited war, the total defeat of the opponent is not a goal. Examples of aims of a limited war are seizing a piece of land, causing the enemy to compromise on a particular issue in negotiations, or simply defending one's own territory. In early December, JCS and State Department discussions regarding fighting a limited war were very tentative. There was a great deal of uncertainty over whether the UNC could actually withstand the Communist onslaught.

In a press conference on 30 November, Truman stated that the USA would 'take any steps necessary to meet the military situation.' When asked if this included the use of the atomic bomb, he replied: 'There has always been active consideration of its use …' Although Truman had no intention of using atomic weapons, the statement greatly frightened Western governments. The British Prime Minister, Clement Attlee, immediately flew to Washington for a meeting with Truman. He and Truman agreed on the need

to fight a limited war and hold the UNC position in Korea as long as possible. The goal of liberating North Korea was abandoned. In the Truman–Attlee communiqué of 8 December, the two leaders called for negotiations with the Communists.

The JCS issued MacArthur a strategic directive on 29 December 1950. It stated that a decisive victory would not be sought in Korea or against the PRC. MacArthur was instructed to hold his position in Korea without risking the safety of his forces. In reply, MacArthur put forth his own strategy of escalation. He called for a blockade of China; air strikes and naval bombardments against China's industry; the reinforcement of the Eighth Army with Chinese Nationalist troops; and diversionary attacks from Taiwan against the Chinese mainland. MacArthur

Ridgway and MacArthur near the front line on 28 January 1951. MacArthur is on the far right. Ridgway stands in the center with sunglasses and a grenade strapped to his shoulder. Unlike MacArthur, Ridgway understood that it was in the best interests of the USA to fight a limited war in Korea. (US Army)

wanted nothing less than to remove the PRC 'as a threat to peace in Asia for generations to come.' The JCS rejected MacArthur's request. Truman personally told MacArthur to avoid actions that might cause a general war.

The Eighth Army commander Walton Walker died on 23 December in a jeep accident. Lieutenant-General Matthew Ridgway replaced him. A renowned airborne commander in the Second World War, outwardly Ridgway seemed a flamboyant character. For example, he always sported a grenade on his webbing. Inwardly, though, Ridgway was extremely thoughtful and perceptive. Ready to adapt to difficult circumstances, he was determined to reinvigorate the Eighth Army and stop the Communists on the ground.

In his first week in Korea, Ridgway toured the front line and visited nearly every divisional commander. Speaking directly with the men at the front, he was overtaken by their demoralization. He wrote in his book, *The Korean War*:

The men I met along the road, those I stopped to talk to and to solicit gripes from – they too all conveyed to me a conviction that this was a bewildered army, not sure of itself or its leaders, not sure what they were doing there, wondering when they would hear the whistle of that homebound transport.

The men were prone to retreating. Because units failed to keep contact with the enemy, Eighth Army intelligence had no idea of the opposing enemy strength. Also, many soldiers were simply not interested in fighting. Civilian life was much more appealing. Veterans, in particular, did not appreciate being called up for a second war in five years. Problems extended beyond the enlisted men to the officers. Ridgway wrote:

The leadership I found in many instances sadly lacking, and I said so out loud. The unwillingness of the army to forgo certain creature comforts, its timidity about getting off scanty roads, its reluctance to move without radio and telephone contact, and its lack of

imagination in dealing with a foe whom they soon outmatched in firepower and dominated in the air and surrounding seas – these were not the fault of the GI . . .

Ridgway immediately acted to revitalize the Eighth Army. He demanded that officers command from the front. Divisional commanders were to be with their forward battalions, and corps commanders were to be with the regiment 'that was in the hottest action.' He ordered commanders to deploy their units off the roads and into the hills. Officers were rebuked for failing to keep contact with the enemy. He forcefully repeated the army slogan: 'Find them! Fix them! Fight them! Finish them!' Officers were also encouraged to breed group cohesion and unit loyalty in their men. To make the army more 'offensive-minded' and certain of their cause, Ridgway issued a general statement to the troops, which said that they were fighting to uphold freedom and fight the slavery of Communism. Ted White, an enlisted man in the African-American 24th US Infantry Regiment, related Ridgway's doctrine from the private soldier's perspective in Rudy Tomedi's book *No Bugles, No Drums*:

We were there to kill Chinese. That's what they told us. The army was done with retreating. General Ridgway was in charge now, and he wasn't a retreating general. We heard it every day from the officers. 'Fix 'em, find 'em, kill 'em.' We went out every day and we attacked. Seems like that's all we did was attack. We hardly ate. We hardly slept. We just attacked. If I'd known what I was getting myself into, I don't know if I'd of [sic] volunteered.

In the midst of these reforms, Ridgway instituted attrition as the new operational doctrine of the Eighth Army. He supported fighting a limited war and understood that warfare had changed since the Second World War. He especially opposed the use of atomic weapons. Instead of annihilating the Communists, he sought to wear down their manpower. To do so, superior UNC firepower was to be exploited to the maximum effect. The hallmark of Ridgway's doctrine of attrition was his directive to his subordinates to maximize enemy casualties while minimizing those of the Eighth Army. Given the daunting Communist numerical superiority, conserving casualties was absolutely crucial. Not a single company was to be sacrificed. There was to be no fighting simply to hold terrain. Rather than fighting the expected Communist attack in forward positions around Seoul, Ridgway intended to withdraw carefully to the Han river.

Ridgway's first use of attrition was successful. Peng launched the Third Phase Offensive in sub-zero conditions on 31 December 1950. Although Ridgway was forced to abandon Seoul, his withdrawal stretched the Communist supply lines to breaking point, forcing Peng to call off the offensive. Ridgway was anxious to seize the initiative. On 15 January 1951, he mounted a reconnaissance in force, Operation Wolfhound, followed by a full-blown counteroffensive, Operation Thunderbolt, 10 days later. In Operation Thunderbolt, the I and IX US Corps made a careful and step-

by-step advance northwards, with heavy artillery and close-air support. The 25th US Division and the renowned Turkish Brigade pummelled the opposing 50th CPV Army in the first day of fighting. Ridgway observed the progress from the air. Frequently, he appeared at corps and divisional headquarters, or even on the front line, to guide and observe operations. By 9 February, the Eighth Army was back on the Han river.

The counteroffensive surprised the CPV commanders, who had not expected such a quick UNC recovery. Overconfident, Mao ordered another attack, the short-lived and ill-advised Fourth Phase Offensive. On 11 February, Chinese forces, led by Deng Hua, broke through the III ROK Corps and threatened the important road hub of Wonju. Further west, the 23rd RCT (2nd US

1. Ridgway's first major counteroffensive was Operation Thunderbolt, which took the Eighth Army back to the Han river by 11 February.
2. Meanwhile, Operation Roundup brought the army forward in the east.
3. From 11 to 20 February, the Eighth Army defeated the Communist Fourth Phase Offensive, after heavy fighting around Wonju and Chipyong-ni.

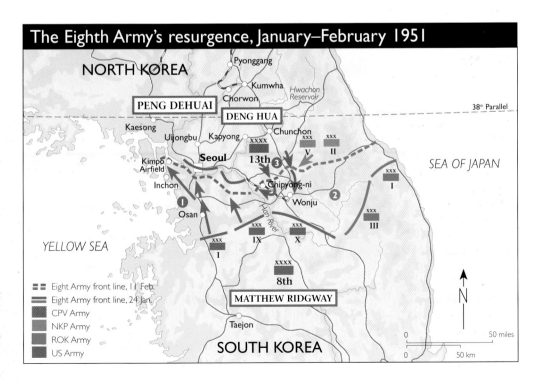

The Eighth Army's resurgence, January–February 1951

Division) and an attached French battalion were encircled at Chipyong-ni. Supplied by air, they fought stubbornly and took the momentum out of the Communist advance. By 20 February, the Communists had been halted at the cost of 17,000 UNC casualties. Communist casualties were probably greater. Because of this defeat, Peng instituted a temporary strategy of withdrawing before UNC attacks in order to conserve his forces before launching another major offensive.

Hoping to bring the Communists to the negotiating table, Ridgway outlined an offensive doctrine for attrition in mid-February. Soldiers often called it 'the meatgrinder.' It was based on the limited objective attack. A limited objective attack was a concentrated and carefully prepared set-piece assault meant to kill Communists, not capture ground. Inflicting the maximum damage on the enemy with the minimum loss to the UNC remained the principle behind all operations. Massive use of superior UNC firepower was emphasized. No attacks would be made in unfavorable or risky

circumstances. Pursuit of the defeated enemy was to be cautious and coordinated, avoiding the kind of reckless advance that had made the Eighth Army vulnerable in November 1950. This also enabled Ridgway to ensure that his forces always had strong logistical support.

In late February and March, Ridgway launched a series of colorfully named limited objective attacks: Operations Killer, Ripper, and Rugged. Due to Peng's new strategy, the Communists generally withdrew and avoided a serious battle. This allowed Ridgway to steadily expand his territorial objectives. UNC units advanced into an empty and devastated Seoul on 14 March. Thereafter, Ridgway and the JCS decided to cross the 38th Parallel in order to secure stronger defensive positions to the

French soldiers on patrol. Their commander, Lieutenant-Colonel Ralph Monclar, had asked to be reduced in rank from lieutenant-general so that he could command the French battalion in Korea. The French served valiantly in several actions, including Chipyong-ni and Heartbreak Ridge. (ECP Armees)

immediate north. The positions subsequently taken became known as the Kansas Line. Sited on strong defensive terrain, it ran along the lower Imjin in the west to Hwachon and then to the east coast, just north of Taepo-ri. The Communists suffered more than 53,000 casualties in Ridgway's limited objective attacks. Total UNC casualties were probably less than 20,000. By now it was clear that Ridgway had turned the Eighth Army into a highly efficient fighting force.

MacArthur never accepted the new strategy of attrition. Indeed, his rhetoric became more inflammatory the further north Ridgway marched. But Ridgway's successes undermined MacArthur's arguments. The advances of the Eighth Army during February and March solidified consensus in Washington that the strategic objective of the UNC was to bring the Communists to the negotiating table through continued attrition.

Aware of the deliberations in Washington, MacArthur issued a statement to the press on 24 March that escalating the war would quickly cause the PRC's military capability to collapse. By advocating a policy contradictory to the one set out by the JCS and the Truman administration, MacArthur was flouting their authority. Then, on 5 April, Senator Joe Martin read a letter from MacArthur in the US House of Representatives. In the letter, MacArthur approved of the idea of landing Chinese Nationalists on the Chinese mainland. He ended the letter with an endorsement of total victory.

Because of these two incidents, Truman acted to relieve MacArthur. Truman wrote in his memoirs:

Time and again General MacArthur had shown that he was unwilling to accept the policies of the Administration. By his repeated public statements he was ... setting his policy against the President's ... If I allowed him to defy the civil authorities in this manner, I myself would be violating my oath to uphold and defend the Constitution.

After some thought, Marshall, Acheson, and the JCS all agreed that MacArthur would have to go. On 14 April, MacArthur was relieved of command of the UNC. Ridgway replaced him, and immediately issued a directive to all of his principal subordinates that no actions were to be taken that risked escalating the conflict.

In early April, Peng was finally ready to launch the major offensive to annihilate the Eighth Army, known as the Fifth Phase Offensive. The plan was for two converging thrusts to break through the UNC line and encircle the Eighth Army divisions one by one. The Third and Nineteenth CPV Army Corps, the western thrust, would cross the Imjin and seize the Seoul–Uijongbu area. Simultaneously, the Ninth and Thirteenth CPV Army Corps, the eastern thrust, would strike in the direction of Kapyong from Kumwha and Hwachon. This was the first action for the Nineteenth and Third CPV Army Corps. They were fully equipped with Soviet weapons, including tanks and artillery. In all, 14 Communist divisions would attack the Eighth Army.

General James Van Fleet replaced Ridgway as commander of the Eighth Army. Van Fleet

General James Van Fleet, Ridgway's successor as commander of the Eighth Army. Van Fleet was an avid proponent of firepower. He espoused massive artillery bombardments, which the troops dubbed the 'Van Fleet Day of Fire.' (National Archives)

had previously commanded the American forces that had assisted the Greek government to defeat Communist guerrillas in the late 1940s. In the west, where the Communist offensive was aimed, Van Fleet had seven divisions (five American) and three brigades at his disposal. Eighth Army operational doctrine remained based on attrition. Without micromanaging, Ridgway supervised Van Fleet's planning. He emphasized that the Eighth Army was to withdraw before the expected Communist offensive. Thereby, the Communists would be exposed to UNC firepower and denied the opportunity to cut off any UNC formations.

On the night of 22 April 1951, the Fifth Phase Offensive began. On the eastern axis of advance, the Ninth CPV Army Corps quickly smashed through the 6th ROK Division. By morning, there was a gaping hole between the 24th US Division to the west and the Marine Division to the east. Elements of the Ninth and Thirteenth CPV Army Corps poured into the gap, threatening to cut off the 24th and 25th US Divisions to the northwest. However, the 27th Commonwealth Brigade conducted a

successful delaying action north of the critical road junction at Kapyong from 23 to 26 April. This prevented the eastern Communist pincer from cutting off any UNC formations.

Meanwhile, the western Communist thrust engaged in a pitched battle to penetrate the

On the night of 22 April, the Communists, intent on annihilating the UNC, launched the Fifth Phase Offensive. The basis of the initial attack was a two-pronged encirclement of the UNC forces in the west.

1. The Ninth and Thirteenth CPV Army Corps smashed through the 6th ROK Division and drove deep into the Eighth Army rear, threatening to encircle the American divisions to the northwest.
2. This caused the 1st Marine Division to quickly refuse their left flank.
3. Meanwhile, the other prong of the offensive, the Nineteenth CPV Army Corps, attacked the 29th British Brigade along the Imjin river, but the Communists were held back until 25 April.
4. Back to the east, the 27th Commonwealth Brigade delayed the Communists at Kapyong from 28 to 30 April, preventing them from encircling any UNC formations.
5. Starting on 25 April, the American divisions threatened with encirclement withdrew toward Seoul.
6. The Eighth Army fell back to the No Name Line, where it halted the Communist advance by 30 April.

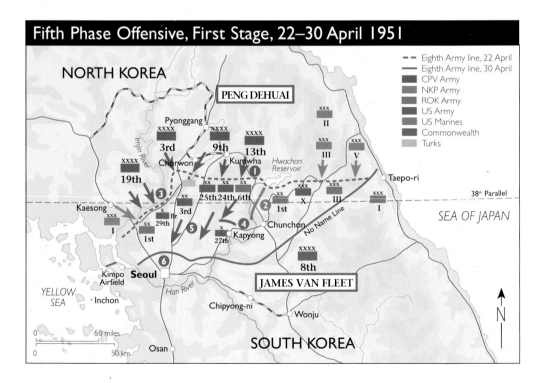

Fifth Phase Offensive, First Stage, 22–30 April 1951

A medic applies first aid while under heavy fire during the Fifth Phase Offensive. (US Army Military History Institute)

UNC line along the Imjin. The focal point of this fighting was the stand of the 1st Battalion, the Gloucestershire Regiment (the Glosters). The Glosters were part of the 29th British Brigade, along with two other British infantry battalions and the 8th King's Royal Irish Hussars. The 8th Royal Irish Hussars was an armored regiment, equipped with the fearsome Centurion tank. Mounting an extremely accurate 20pdr (83.4mm) gun, the Centurion was debatably the best tank in the world. The British units contained a mix of regular soldiers and conscripted National Servicemen. These were steady and professional troops. Known as two of the most reliable formations in the Eighth Army, the two Commonwealth brigades had been repeatedly assigned to vital rearguard actions.

The 29th British Brigade, commanded by Brigadier Thomas Brodie, was disposed directly behind the Imjin, guarding two crossings. The brigade was under the direct authority of Major-General Robert Soule, commander of the 3rd US Infantry Division. The British were the hinge between the 1st ROK Division on the lower Imjin and the American divisions to the northeast. If the Chinese annihilated the British, the 3rd and 25th US Divisions would be outflanked. This was indeed the goal of the

Nineteenth CPV Army Corps. The army corps' advance depended upon the quick annihilation of the 29th British Brigade.

The Glosters, commanded by Lieutenant-Colonel James Carne, were located on the western flank of the British line. On the night of 22 April, the Chinese surged over the Imjin at 'Gloster Crossing.' Carne could not retreat without uncovering the flanks of the British battalion to the east and the 1st ROK Division to the west. The Chinese attacked the Glosters' positions four times in two and a half hours. Mortar, artillery, and Vickers machine-gun fire inflicted heavy losses on the attackers. The Glosters lost no ground and suffered few casualties. The rest of the 29th British Brigade was also attacked.

On the evening of 23 April, increasing pressure forced the Glosters to withdraw from their position before 'Gloster Crossing' to the nearby Hill 235, dubbed 'Gloucester Hill.' However, the Chinese had infiltrated almost completely around Gloucester Hill. On the afternoon of 24 April, Soule asked Brodie about the Glosters' situation. Brodie replied: 'A bit sticky; things are pretty sticky down there.' To the subtle British, 'pretty sticky' meant critical. But to forthright Americans, it merely meant unpleasant. Therefore, Soule ordered the Glosters to continue to hold. On Gloucester Hill, the Chinese attacked from three directions throughout that night. Engaged in close combat with the Chinese,

the British repeatedly called artillery fire down upon their own positions. The Glosters' ranks were filled with wounded men who would not leave the firing line. By morning, ammunition was nearly exhausted.

With the Communists threatening to break through all along his line, Lieutenant-General Frank Milburn, commander of the I US Corps, finally ordered a general withdrawal on the morning of 25 April. Unfortunately, Soule and Brodie lacked the reserves to break the Glosters out. Brodie ordered the battalion to disperse and try to escape in small independent parties. Only 39 men made it back to UNC lines. The rest, including Carne, were killed or taken prisoner. The remainder of the 29th British Brigade successfully withdrew from the Imjin. Supported by a squadron of Centurions, the infantry cut through the Communists attempting to block the line of retreat.

The Glosters' stand blunted the western Communist thrust. The Nineteenth CPV Army Corps had been delayed for three vital days. Human wave attacks exposed the Chinese to devastating losses from British and American firepower. One of the divisions of the attacking 63rd CPV Army was entirely destroyed. The 29th British Brigade lost 1,091 men in the three days of fighting. Approximately half of these casualties were borne by the Glosters.

A sketch by Bryande Grineau of the last stand of 1st Battalion, the Gloucestershire Regiment, on the Imjin. The stand enabled several American divisions to escape encirclement, but most of the battalion was killed or taken prisoner in the process. Van Fleet called it 'the most outstanding example of unit bravery in modern warfare.' (Illustrated London News)

Shortly thereafter, Van Fleet ordered the I and IX US Corps to fall back 25 miles (40km) to the No Name Line before Seoul. When the Chinese advanced again, they could not dislodge the entrenched and prepared UNC forces. Van Fleet later said that the loss of the Glosters had been necessary to save the whole Eighth Army. Nevertheless, the destruction of an entire battalion outraged Ridgway. It violated his basic dictum of never ordering units to hold a position at all costs.

In early May, Peng shifted his weight for a second blow in the eastern half of the peninsula. The Ninth and Third CPV Army Corps were transferred east to attack alongside the II and V North Korean Corps. On 16 May, the Communists slammed into the III ROK Corps and the adjacent ROK divisions of the X US Corps. The III ROK Corps was virtually annihilated and fled south. In accordance with Van Fleet's orders, the X US Corps fell back. This extended Communist supply lines and provided time to move UNC reinforcements into the front

These riflemen of the 65th Regimental Combat Team (RCT), 3rd US Division, are participating in the UNC counterattacks to the Fifth Phase Offensive. The 65th RCT was composed almost entirely of Puerto Ricans. (US Army Military History Institute)

line. Intense artillery fire and close air support inflicted heavy casualties on the exposed Communist forces. On 21 May, running out of food and ammunition, the Communist advance ground to a halt.

Ridgway was intent on exploiting the Communists' defeat and forcing them to come to the negotiating table. The Eighth Army counterattacked across the front on 20 May. UNC spearheads cut Communist lines of retreat. Many Chinese panicked and large numbers of prisoners were taken. Tzo Peng, a machine-gunner, said that the situation was pure chaos and that there was nothing to eat for five days. He found the shelling horrifying. Unable to fight or escape, he surrendered. The Eighth Army had

recaptured the Kansas Line by 15 June. Additionally, the lower half of the Iron Triangle was seized. The Iron Triangle was the road and rail complex connecting Pyonggang, Chorwon, and Kumwha. Its unique position made it the communications hub between the Communist front line and the rest of North Korea. Thus, it was a major Communist supply center. The extension of the UNC line in this area was known as the Wyoming Line.

Ridgway did not press the offensive further because he believed that the price of advancing to Pyongyang or the Yalu would be too great. The rugged terrain of North Korea was optimal for a strong Communist defensive. UNC supply lines would become extended while the Communists drew nearer to their supply centers on the Yalu. Furthermore, there was the risk that such an action would cause the PRC or even the Soviet Union to escalate the war.

The Fifth Phase Offensive was the most important battle of the Korean War. The

Fifth Phase Offensive, Second Stage, 16–20 May 1951

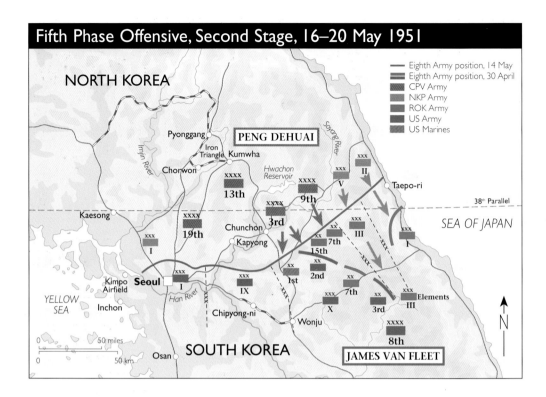

After being defeated in the west, the Communists shifted their offensive to the east. They effected a major breakthrough, but the planned UNC withdrawal caused their advance to quickly lose momentum and grind to a halt.

UNC lost about 25,000 men, followed by another 14,700 in the counteroffensive operations in June. These were heavy losses. However, the Communists suffered at least 85,000 casualties. This does not include numbers for the UNC counteroffensive, in which the UNC captured 17,000 prisoners and probably killed or wounded many more than that. The defeat caused a major change in Chinese strategy. Mao realized that the losses incurred since January meant that the UNC could not be decisively defeated. Rather, he decided that cease-fire negotiations were now acceptable. Stalin agreed. Since 31 May, representatives of the USA and the Soviet Union had been tentatively discussing the possibility of commencing cease-fire negotiations. On 23 June 1951, Jacob Malik, the Soviet Ambassador to the UN, implied in the UN radio program The Price of Peace that

the Communists would accept negotiations. Notwithstanding this decision, Mao and Peng were intent on winning more victories on the battlefield before actually agreeing to a cease-fire. Nevertheless, the Communists' willingness to enter into negotiations and fight a limited war marked the abandonment of their goal of reunifying Korea. While it did not end the war immediately, the UNC victory in the Fifth Phase Offensive laid the basis for a negotiated settlement to the conflict.

Negotiations

Cease-fire negotiations began on 10 July 1951 behind Communist lines at Kaesong. No political issues were to be discussed, only 'military' issues related to the initiation of a cease-fire. Vice-Admiral C. Turner Joy headed the UNC delegation. North Korean General Nam Il led the Communist delegation. However, Stalin, Mao, and the JCS were intimately involved in negotiations and controlled the bargaining positions of their respective delegations. The final agenda was

The UNC delegation to the cease-fire negotiations. From left to right are Major-General Henry Hodes, Major-General Laurence Craigie, Vice-Admiral C. Turner Joy, Major-General Paik Sun Yup, and Rear-Admiral Arleigh Burke. Joy was the head UNC delegate. (Defence Department)

confirmed on 26 July. It comprised five items: first, the adoption of an agenda; second, the establishment of a cease-fire line; third, supervisory arrangements for the cease-fire; fourth, the exchange of prisoners of war (POWs); and, fifth, recommendations for a political settlement of the conflict. In the process of establishing a final agenda, the UNC delegation had prevented the Communists from including one of their basic demands, the mutual withdrawal of foreign troops from Korea, as an item. The negotiators then turned to discussing Item Two, which seemed to be the most important issue on the agenda.

Given the new context of negotiating while fighting, Ridgway updated his strategy. Attrition would now be used to enforce the UNC bargaining position by increasing the

The Communist delegation to the cease-fire negotiations. From left to right are: Major-General Hsieh Fang and Lieutenant-General Deng Hua, the Chinese delegates; and then, General Nam Il, Major-General Lee Sang Cho, and General Chang Pyong San, the North Korean delegates. Nam Il was the main Communist spokesman. (Defence Department)

costs of war for the Communists. The Kansas–Wyoming Line would be the foundation of the Eighth Army's defensive positions and the basis for a cease-fire line. Limited objective attacks would take small portions of ground in order to wear down the Communists and make minor improvements in the Eighth Army's defensive positions. As before, Ridgway took careful steps to ensure that no actions were taken that might be costly or escalate the conflict. In particular, he vetoed several ambitious plans advocated by Van Fleet for a major offensive to the waist of Korea.

With the initiation of negotiations, Mao and Peng adopted a doctrine of attrition on the battlefield. Given the virtually inexhaustible Chinese manpower supply, Mao and Peng believed that the USA could never defeat China in a war of attrition. Like the UNC, the Communists' goal for attrition was to enforce their bargaining position. Tactically, human wave attacks were abandoned. Instead, Peng endorsed 'small-scale annihilation' – methodically destroying individual enemy battalions. He particularly sought to engage in 'see-saw battles.' In a 'see-saw battle,' the

Communists would attack a certain UNC position repeatedly until they held it, regardless of how many times UNC forces counterattacked and recaptured the position. Even if they suffered heavier losses than the UNC in the ebb and flow of a 'see-saw battle,' the Communist commanders believed that their superior manpower would make the UNC relatively worse off. The Communists also fortified their front line and increased their strength in artillery.

Negotiations proceeded very slowly at Kaesong. The Communists wanted the 38th Parallel to be the cease-fire line. The UNC and USA, on the other hand, wanted the current front line – the line of contact – to be the cease-fire line. The rugged terrain along the Kansas–Wyoming Line was much more defensible than the flat ground along the 38th Parallel. As a temporary bargaining ploy, the UNC delegation initially called for a line north of this, within current

Men of the 3rd US Division advance upon a hill held by the Chinese during the summer fighting of 1951. The smoke rising from the hill is the result of the preceding artillery bombardment. American assaults received intense artillery support. (US Army)

Communist positions. This only made the Communist delegation more obstinate. The following quote from 14 August is a good example of Nam Il's rhetoric:'We stand firm for making the 38th Parallel the military demarcation line because it reflects the military and is hence fair and reasonable. We oppose resolutely your proposal of pushing the military demarcation line completely into our positions because it is absurd, arrogant, and intolerable.' Unshakably somber, the Communists would even insult the UNC delegates as a means of rejecting their demands. This negotiating style was infuriating to the UNC delegation.

By mid-August, the Eighth Army's limited objective attacks had convinced the Chinese that military action to seize the 38th Parallel was impossible. Nevertheless, Stalin and Mao preferred to continue fighting, in hopes of an improvement in Communist fortunes. The Communist delegation suspended negotiations on 23 August because of supposed UNC violations of the neutral zone around Kaesong. The next two months would be consumed by tangential discussions between UNC general headquarters and the Communists over where and how to reconvene negotiations.

Ridgway intensified limited objective attacks in the fall of 1951 in order to increase the pressure on the Communists to concede on Item Two. These offensives mauled the Communist armies. In the process, the Eighth Army suffered substantial, if sustainable, losses. This was particularly the case in a series of slogging matches around the Punchbowl, Bloody Ridge, and Heartbreak Ridge – terrain features on the eastern half of the peninsula. Determined to capture Communist positions overlooking the Eighth Army front line, Van Fleet was induced into fighting just the sort of 'see-saw battle' that Peng had planned for, with the same pieces of terrain changing hands repeatedly. By the end of the fighting in October, the Eighth Army had suffered 8,000 casualties, 3,300 of which fell on the

Bloody Ridge, the scene of a massive 'see-saw battle' between the North Koreans and the 2nd US Division in August and September 1951. (US Army)

South Korean laborers bringing supplies to the front. They are carrying the ubiquitous Korean A-Frame backpack. (US Military History Institute)

The fall offensives, September–October 1951

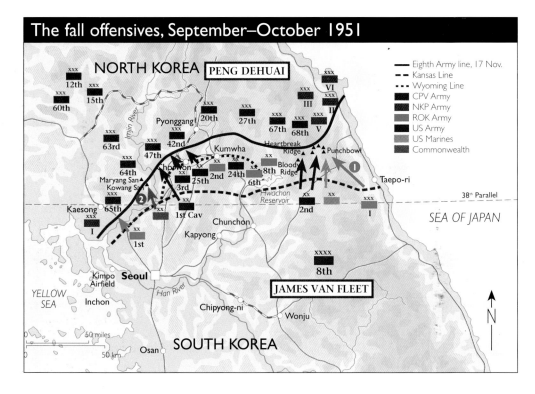

In the fall of 1951, the Eighth Army pressed the Communists back in a series grinding offensives. This map shows the two most important.

1. From July to October, the I ROK Corps, Marine Division, and 2nd US Division engaged in a series of slogging matches over possession of terrain features known as the Punchbowl, Bloody Ridge, and Heartbreak Ridge.
2. From 3 to 18 October, several UNC divisions wore down the Communists and seized dominating terrain to the north in Operation Commando.

2nd US Division alone. Communist losses were probably much greater due to the immense firepower of the Eighth Army.

The most effective of the fall offensives was Operation Commando. In addition to wearing down the Communists, Ridgway and Van Fleet wanted to seize a range of steep hills north of the Imjin, known as the Jamestown Line. The line formed excellent defensive positions because there was no dominating terrain to the immediate north. Three divisions of the I US Corps and one of the IX US Corps would mount the attack. They would be opposed by the 47th and 64th CPV Armies. One of the I US Corps'

attacking divisions would be the 1st Commonwealth Division. Its operations in Operation Commando would epitomize Ridgway's dictum of maximizing enemy casualties while minimizing one's own.

In July 1951, the 25th Canadian Brigade, the 28th Commonwealth Brigade, and the 29th British Brigade joined to form the 1st Commonwealth Division. The formation of the division united the Commonwealth ground forces in Korea. As noted above, Commonwealth infantry was of a very high caliber. The division also boasted a strong and highly professional artillery arm and the armored support of the 8th Royal Irish Hussars. There was even an Indian Field Ambulance unit.

The Commonwealth Division's objectives were Hills 235, 355 (Kowang San), and 317 (Maryang San). With steep faces, they were the most difficult objectives of all the attacking divisions. The attack began on 3 October. The 28th Commonwealth Brigade assaulted Kowang San and Maryang San, defended by the 191st CPV Division. The Communists held well-entrenched and in-depth positions. The

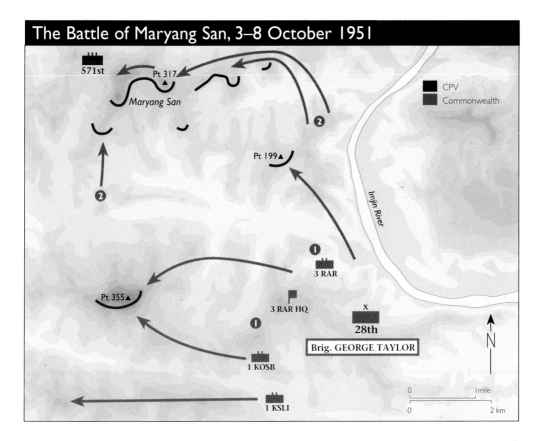

The Battle of Maryang San, 3–8 October 1951

As a part of Operation Commando, the 28th Commonwealth Brigade seized the highpoints of Maryang San and Kowang San.

1. On 4 October, the 3rd Battalion, Royal Australian Regiment (3 RAR) seized Pt 199, in preparation for the advance on Maryang San. Additionally, an Australian company outflanked Kowang San, while the 1st Battalion, the King's Own Scottish Borderers Regiment attacked frontally.
2. The next day, the 3 RAR took the Maryang San ridgeline from the flank, while the 1st Battalion, the Royal Northumberland Fusiliers Regiment pressed the Chinese front.

ridges were lined with covered trenches, bunkers, and dug-in artillery batteries. One hundred and thirty guns and heavy mortars supported the attack, including those of the 16th Field Regiment, Royal New Zealand Artillery. The 3rd Battalion, the Royal Australian Regiment (3 RAR), commanded by Lieutenant-Colonel Frank Hassett, spearheaded the assault. Ever since Gallipoli, the Australians had enjoyed a reputation for fighting hard, innovating quickly, and being more cunning

than the enemy. For the operation, Hassett espoused bold flanking movements along ridgelines – a tactic learned fighting the Japanese in New Guinea – in order to attack the Chinese from unexpected directions.

The Australians smashed through the Chinese defenses, first outflanking Kowang San and then Maryang San from the east, while two British battalions held the fronts of these positions. The fighting was very intense. The New Zealanders expended 50,000 rounds in support of the operation. Centurions fired directly on the Chinese from the Commonwealth starting positions. The following quote by Lieutenant Maurie Pears, from the book *Korea Remembered*, illustrates the combined-arms and infiltration tactics used in the final assault on Maryang San:

C Company was to rush across the valley and move through B and D Companies, which were held up under Point 317, to take the summit from the rear. Surprise was again the tactic, the

The British Centurion tank; arguably the finest tank in the world during the Korean War. Its 20pdr gun was extremely accurate. Its ability to knock out T-34s emplaced in the Communist lines was renowned. (The Tank Museum, Bovington)

Chinese being used to the previous massed frontal attacks of the Americans. The battalion artillery and tanks would support us with enfilade fire during the final assault, as the approaches to the summit were clear from the observation post.

Once successful, the Australians quickly consolidated and dug-in on the Maryang San ridgeline. The ensuing Chinese counterattacks were repulsed, causing the 191st CPV Division to withdraw. In these counterattacks, the Australians withstood some of the heaviest Communist artillery concentrations of the war. The Australians had destroyed two enemy battalions and captured 50 prisoners. There were 109 Australian casualties. Along the rest of the line, the remaining attacking UNC divisions were also successful after vigorous fighting.

The Communists launched a major counteroffensive to retake the ground lost to the I and IX US Corps. On 4 November, two CPV regiments with heavy artillery support fell on Maryang San, now held by the 1st Battalion, the King's Own Scottish Borderers Regiment. Rather than suffer exorbitant casualties in a see-saw battle, the battalion fell back to Kowang San. There, the Commonwealth Division, with its formidable firepower, decimated the attackers from

Australians on the march. In addition to air and naval commitments, Australia deployed the 3rd Battalion, Royal Australian Regiment, to Korea in 1950, followed by the 1st Battalion in 1952. (Australian War Memorial)

strong in-depth positions. Thus, despite the loss of Maryang San, the Commonwealth Division maximized Chinese casualties while minimizing its own. Since 3 October, the division had suffered 1,159 casualties. Chinese casualties are unknown, but probably were much greater, given the futility of their attacks. The Chinese made no significant headway against the UNC elsewhere either. By mid-November, the 47th and 64th CPV Armies were exhausted and had to be withdrawn from the front line.

More importantly, just four days after the start of Operation Commando, the Communists indicated their willingness to reopen negotiations. On 21 October, the two delegations finally agreed to resume negotiations at Panmunjom, a new neutral site located between the two front lines. As negotiations reopened, Mao decided to accept the line of contact as the cease-fire line. The UNC was not about to crack and the costs of war for the Chinese were rising. Additionally, the rugged ground on the line of contact bore defensive advantages for the Communists, just as it did for the UNC. However, Kaesong was an obstacle to agreement. Ridgway and Joy wanted it on the UNC side of the cease-fire line, even though it was not in their military possession.

Over Ridgway's objection, the JCS offered a compromise on 17 November. It stipulated that the current front line would be frozen as the actual cease-fire line as long as agreement was reached on the remaining agenda items within 30 days. Thereafter, the line of contact would become the cease-fire line. Subsequently, on 27 November, the two sides reached agreement on Item Two. This essentially created a de facto one-month truce because further offensives served no territorial purpose.

Unfortunately, the impact of the fall offensives was not enough to end the war. Discussion on Item Three, supervisory arrangements for the cease-fire, stalled over the composition of an armistice commission and the number of airfields permitted in North Korea after the war. To overcome the impasse, attention shifted to Item Four, the return of POWs. However, negotiations quickly stalled here as well. Meanwhile, a stalemate appeared on the battlefield. Neither side engaged in major offensive operations. In spite of their recent military successes, American leaders were reluctant to return to an intense operational tempo because of the heavy casualties incurred in the offensives since July. The Communists, on the other hand, had been greatly weakened by the fall offensives and focused on rebuilding their forces.

The air war

While the Eighth Army fought the Communists on the ground, dramatic battles were being fought in the air. The Korean War was the first jet war and the one occasion in the Cold War where American and Soviet military forces regularly engaged each other in combat.

From July to November 1951, the UNC conducted air operations as if fighting a total war. The North Korean air force was immediately swept from the air, and bombers directly targeted North Korea's industry. However, once the Chinese intervened, the war in the air became limited. There was a tacit understanding that the Communists would not bomb Japan, South Korea, or UNC naval forces as long as the UNC did not strike Chinese or Soviet territory. With MacArthur's dismissal, the JCS delineated explicit restrictions on air operations. Aircraft were forbidden from flying within 3 miles (5km) of China and 20 miles (32km) of the Soviet Union. China could only be struck in retaliation to a major Communist attack, and targets on the Yalu were off-limits without Ridgway's explicit permission.

In spite of these restrictions, several US politicians and military officers frequently called for Communist airfields in Manchuria to be bombed. Although contingency plans existed to do so, the JCS never authorized the strikes for two main reasons. First, there was the continuing fear that attacking China would escalate the war. Second, the USA and UNC actually lacked the capability to fight an air war over China. It would require stripping the other US commands, including in Europe, of aircraft. Aircraft losses would certainly be high, weakening the global Western military position.

Recent evidence suggests that a large percentage of the air-to-air combat of the Korean War involved Soviet pilots. Some historians even believe that the Chinese effort was a mere sideshow. Over 200 of the best Soviet aircraft, pilots, and crews were stationed in Andong, China. Several had experience flying in the Second World War and more than a few were aces. Stalin was adamant that no Soviet pilot be captured. The Russians dressed in Chinese uniforms and flew aircraft with Chinese or North Korean markings. One of their major roles was equipping and training the PLA air force. The Chinese flew out of air bases in northern China and North Korea. The PLA air force did not begin major air operations until September 1951. From then until the end of the war, the Chinese always deployed three divisions (135 MiG-15s) into combat. Additionally, the Communists possessed

hundreds of MiG-15s in reserve.

Communist air operations focused on fighting for air supremacy over North Korea. Virtually the only bombing missions were night-time harassment of the UNC front line by Polikarpov Po-2 biplanes, known as 'Bed-check Charlies.' The MiG-15 jet fighter was the primary Communist aircraft. It was an outstanding fighter. Its swept wings enabled great speed and maneuverability. Additionally, it could operate at high altitudes around 40,000 feet (12,000m) and had a strong rate of climb. A combination of one 37mm and two 20mm cannons provided armament.

The US Far East Air Force (FEAF) conducted most of the UNC air operations. The FEAF employed an assortment of aircraft. Many were propeller-driven stalwarts of the Second World War. In the beginning of the war, F-51 Mustangs were still being used in an air superiority role. With its large payload

A MiG-15 in take-off. With this fighter, the Communists challenged the UNC for air supremacy over MiG Alley. Swept wings gave the fighter high speed and maneuverability. (US Air Force)

and long range, the B-29 Stratofortress was the mainstay of the FEAF bomber force. The B-26 Invader served in close support, interdiction, and strategic bombing roles where more accuracy was needed. Two new jet aircraft were the F-80 Shooting Star and F-84 Thunderjet. Both were straight-winged, heavy, and reliable. Although they could be employed in a fighter role, the FEAF preferred to use them as fighter-bombers because of their inferiority to the MiG-15. Additionally, the South Africans and Australians each contributed a squadron of Mustangs that were eventually upgraded to Sabres and Gloster Meteors (a British jet) respectively.

Only the US F-86 Sabre, the sole UNC aircraft with swept wings, could equal the MiG-15. Designed as a fighter-bomber, the Sabre was heavy, durable, stable, and easy to fly. In general, the two aircraft were evenly matched. At high speeds, the Sabre was more maneuverable and easier to handle than the MiG-15. However, the Sabre could neither climb as fast nor fly as high as the MiG-15. Furthermore, its six .50 caliber machine-guns lacked the stopping power of the MiG-15's cannons. The USA's most important advantage in the Korean War, though, was the superior training and experience of its fighter pilots. The UNC had more pilots with extensive experience fighting over Europe or the Pacific during the Second World War than the Communists had.

In November 1950, the first MiG-15s (Soviets) appeared over North Korea. They established control over the northwest corner of North Korea between the Chongchon and Yalu rivers. This area would become infamously known as MiG Alley. The FEAF regularly sortied into MiG Alley to protect their bombers and challenge the Communists for air supremacy. Both the Sabre and the MiG-15 had a low combat radius. However, due to Communist strategy, the MiG-15s were always a short distance from their bases over the Yalu. The Sabres, on the other hand, flew from South Korea and could patrol in MiG Alley for a very limited amount of time. A common Communist tactic was to dive in on Sabres from above,

fire a few bursts, and then streak back to safety across the Yalu. In spite of strict orders to the contrary, Sabre pilots often chased fleeing MiG-15s across the Yalu in 'hot pursuit.'

Air-to-air combat tactics had not changed significantly since the Second World War. Jet engines simply made everything happen much faster. A pilot's objective in air-to-air combat was still to hold a commanding position over an opponent long enough to shoot him down with gunfire at a range of 1,000 feet (300m) or less. The basic tactical rule was that each individual aircraft paired up with a wingman to provide support. Using this sound tactic, Sabre squadrons would try to break up Communist formations and shoot down the MiG-15s one by one. However, the Sabres were always fighting an outnumbered battle. General Otto Weyland, commander of the FEAF, repeatedly requested more Sabre squadrons. But Air Force Chief of Staff Hoyt Vandenberg could not deploy significant Sabre reinforcements to Korea without dangerously weakening American military strength elsewhere in the world.

Interdiction, the disruption of an enemy's lines of communications, became the primary FEAF bombing mission in early 1951 when it was necessary to limit the supply of the Communist forces advancing into South Korea. At that time, interdiction was highly effective because the Communists required an intense rate of supply to sustain their offensives. Bombing bridges and roads overburdened the already elongated Communist supply lines.

Interdiction intensified in May 1951 when the FEAF initiated Operation Strangle. Weyland agreed with Ridgway's strategy of using military force to coerce the Communists. Given its success earlier in the year, he believed that interdiction would be the most effective means of doing so. Initially, Operation Strangle started as a short campaign against Communist supply lines within 60 miles (100km) of the front. But in August 1951, the operation was extended in both length and scope to target bridges, rail

A flight of four F-86 Sabres. The Sabre handled better than the MiG-15 at high speeds and was more resilient. The true edge that American fighter pilots possessed, though, was their extensive training and combat experience from the Second World War. (US Air Force)

tracks, and locomotives throughout North Korea. The object of these operations was to increase the long-term costs of supplying their front line and force the Communists either to accept UNC terms in the truce talks or to retreat further north.

Partly as a response to Operation Strangle, the Communists pressed their numerical advantage in a major fighter offensive in the fall of 1951. This marked the entry of the Chinese into the air war in force. The Soviets coordinated their activities with the Chinese and matched the number of aircraft they deployed into major air battles. American pilots found that the inexperienced Chinese were very brave but lacked skill. The Soviets received more respect. Occasionally, a lone Soviet pilot would tangle with the Sabres,

showing off his skill and daring. The Americans used the term 'honcho' to describe such pilots.

On 18 October, Weyland initiated daylight bombing raids into MiG Alley to thwart Communist airfield construction. The Superfortresses could not be effectively protected from intercepting MiG-15s. Exploiting their ability to fly at high altitudes, the MiG-15 pilots would dive through the fighter screen, fire upon the bombers, and then escape across the Yalu.

A few bursts from their cannon had a devastating effect on the bombers. The black day for FEAF Bomber Command came on 23 October. Fifty MiG-15s intercepted nine B-29 Superfortress bombers attacking Namsi airfield. Three bombers were destroyed. Another eight received major damage. With a total force of only 90 operational Superfortresses, continued losses at this rate would be catastrophic. Therefore, at the end of October, Superfortress daylight bombing raids were

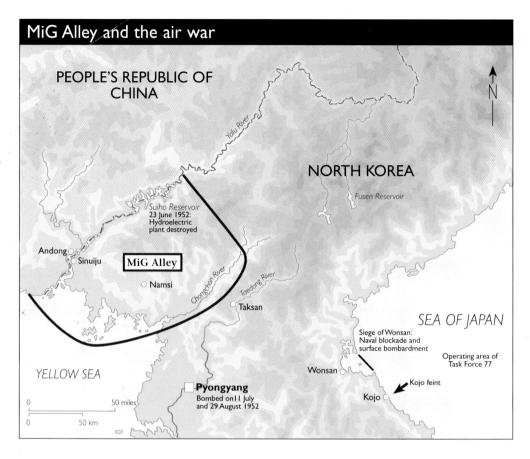

MiG Alley and the air war

PEOPLE'S REPUBLIC OF CHINA

Yalu River

NORTH KOREA

Fusen Reservoir

Suiho Reservoir
23 June 1952:
Hydroelectric
plant destroyed

Andong
Sinuiju

MiG Alley

Namsi

Chongchon River

Taedong River

Taksan

SEA OF JAPAN

Siege of Wonsan:
Naval blockade and
surface bombardment

Operating area of
Task Force 77

Wonsan

YELLOW SEA

Kojo feint

Pyongyang
Bombed on 11 July
and 29 August 1952

Kojo

0   50 miles
0   50 km

N

MiG Alley was the area of North Korean air space in which the Communists fought for air superiority.

permanently abandoned. Weyland eventually curtailed all fighter-bomber operations in MiG Alley as well.

Nevertheless, in spite of increased Sabre losses, superior American tactics were defeating the MiG-15s in most air-to-air engagements. The Communists finally abandoned their air offensive after 13 December. On that day, 150 MiG-15s attacked the Sabres flying in MiG Alley. The Communists lost 13 jets. These losses cooled their enthusiasm for major air battles. The end result of the offensive was that the Communists held air superiority within MiG Alley over FEAF bombers and fighter-bombers but not the Sabres.

Fighting continued in MiG Alley for the remainder of the war. There was another set of major air battles in the late summer and

early fall of 1952. These did not alter the USA's tactical dominance. Chinese skill in air-to-air combat improved as the war progressed, but superior American tactics and experience continued to win most engagements.

When limited objective attacks were suspended after the agreement on Item Two, UNC general headquarters and the JCS looked to air power as a means to coerce the Communists without the high costs of offensive ground operations. Consequently, in the first half of 1952, Operation Strangle was the focus of UNC military operations. However, Operation Strangle was not a success. In a period of static warfare, the Communist forces did not require the high rate of supply that had been necessary during their offensive operations in the first half of 1951.

Moreover, the FEAF was unable to inflict serious permanent damage on the

Communist supply system. This was not the age of smart weapons. Piloting a high-speed aircraft through heavy flak and planting a dumb bomb on a rail track a few feet wide was no easy task. The Communists were also adept at repairing and preventing damage to their supply lines. Destroyed bridges were quickly rebuilt, and cut roads and railroad tracks were bypassed. Obvious targets, like bridges, were surrounded with anti-aircraft guns.

The economic cost of Operation Strangle was unsustainable. The UNC lost 330 aircraft in the operation. The cost of losing a high-performance aircraft far offset the cost that the Communists incurred in repairing a dirt road, steel rail track, or concrete bridge. Meanwhile, the Communist front line became stronger than ever. By 1952 an impressive amount of tanks, artillery pieces, and ammunition supplies were positioned at the front.

When the failure of Operation Strangle became clear, FEAF headquarters began searching for a new strategy. In April 1952,

two staff officers in FEAF headquarters, Colonel Richard Randolph and Lieutenant-Colonel Ben Mayo, created the sustained air pressure strategy, which envisioned concentrated strikes against key North Korean industrial and political targets. This would severely damage the North Korean industrial base and undermine civilian morale. It was hoped that this damage would translate into concessions at the negotiating table. Randolph and Mayo's superior, General Jacob Smart, FEAF Deputy for Operations, enthusiastically advocated the plan.

General Mark Clark replaced Ridgway as commander of the UNC on 12 May 1952. Outwardly, Clark supported the American strategy of limited war, but inwardly he believed that much more drastic measures were required to coerce the Communists. Accordingly, Clark, along with Weyland,

A fantastic picture of a napalm strike against a marshaling yard in North Korea. Most interdiction strikes were not this effective. Small rail tracks, bridges, and roads were very difficult to hit with a dumb bomb. (US Air Force)

strongly endorsed the sustained air pressure strategy.

On 23 June 1952, the first strikes of the new strategy were conducted against North Korean hydroelectric plants at Kojo, Fusen, Kyosen, and Suiho. These plants provided power to virtually all of North Korea and much of Manchuria. Suiho, on the Yalu, was the fourth largest hydroelectric facility in the world. All four plants were severely damaged. Power was reportedly lost throughout North Korea. The UNC continued striking these and other plants as the North Koreans scrambled to get them back into operation.

On 11 July, the sustained air pressure campaign entered its next stage when the FEAF, along with Australian Meteors and Royal Navy strike aircraft, bombed Pyongyang. Pyongyang was struck again on 29 August, in the largest air raid of the Korean War (1,403 sorties). Although both raids were directed against military targets, tremendous collateral damage leveled Pyongyang. Several targets were napalmed. Kim told Stalin that 6,000 civilians had been killed. International outrage accompanied the attack. The British were

particularly upset that they had not been briefed on the raid.

After Pyongyang, Smart focused the sustained air pressure campaign on the remnants of North Korea's industry. North Korea's extensive mining facilities were especially targeted. Oil refineries and the remaining power plants were also hit. But as 1952 drew to a close, the number of important industrial and political targets was rapidly dwindling. Therefore, operations focused on striking major supply points and providing close-air support.

The sustained air pressure strategy was largely a success. UNC air losses were significantly reduced and severe damage was dealt to the North Korean industrial base. Soon after it had begun, Kim and Mao began asking Stalin about the possibility of agreeing to an armistice. However, there were two major drawbacks to the sustained air pressure strategy. First, most of the industry vital to the Communist war effort was located in the Soviet Union and China, not North Korea. Second, North Korea itself was relatively unindustrialized and did not contain a large number of high-value targets. In general, the sustained air pressure strategy represented a gradual weakening rather than a significant reduction in Communist military capability. It alone could not coerce the Communists to concede.

The naval war

Naval operations formed an important, if peripheral, role in UNC operations. Command of the sea ensured that the UNC had a secure line of communications to Japan and the USA. The US Seventh Fleet, centered on Task Force 77, primarily

General Mark Clark replaced Ridgway as Supreme Commander of the UNC on 12 May 1952. Clark had commanded the US army in Italy during the Second World War. In Korea, he did not like the idea of fighting a limited war but loyally obeyed JCS instructions. (Defence Department)

FEAF and US Navy fighter-bombers struck the Suiho hydroelectric plant, the fourth largest in the world, on 23 June 1952. It was the opening strike of the new sustained air pressure strategy, which sought to coerce the Communists by destroying valuable industrial and military targets. (Defence Deparment)

operated off the east coast of Korea. The Commonwealth navies, based around the Royal Navy Far East Fleet, usually including a British aircraft carrier, operated in the Yellow Sea. For four months, the Royal Australian

The battleship USS *New Jersey* fires a 16-inch broadside at targets near the 38th Parallel. One Iowa-class battleship was always deployed with Task Force 77. They frequently engaged in gunnery duels with North Korean coastal artillery around Wonsan. (Defence Department)

Navy's aircraft carrier HMAS *Sydney* also participated in these operations.

With varying degrees of success, the UNC naval command tried to translate its command of the sea into effectiveness in the land war. The guns of American cruisers and battleships could strike far inland. Shore bombardment interdicted supply lines and provided support fire for the ground units of the Eighth Army. Eighth Army soldiers often commented upon the accuracy and devastating effect of the 16-inch guns of the Iowa-class battleships. British, Australian, and American destroyers and frigates engaged small Communist craft, conducted bombardments, and supported commando raids in the shallows and small islands along Korea's littoral. Naval forces kept Wonsan in a state of virtual siege. In October 1952, the Seventh Fleet even

conducted an amphibious feint at Kojo, just south of Wonsan.

Task Force 77 was intimately involved in both Operation Strangle and the sustained air pressure strategy. Task Force 77 generally consisted of two Essex-class fleet carriers conducting air operations, a third replenishing at sea, and a fourth in port in Japan. Their aircraft participated in the attacks on Suiho power station and Pyongyang. The carriers were uniquely able to launch strikes from anywhere off North Korea's coast and hit targets inaccessible to

the land-based FEAF. For example, the largest naval strike of the war was against the Aoji oil refinery on 1 September 1952. Eight miles (13km) from the Soviet frontier, only aircraft from Task Force 77 could get within range of the target with minimal risk of violating Soviet territory.

There were three main types of naval aircraft: the F-4U Corsair, AD Skyraider, and F-9F Panther. The gull-winged F-4U Corsair was a renowned fighter from the Pacific War. In Korea, it served primarily as a fighter-bomber and was the principal aircraft

The USS *Valley Forge* (CV-45), an Essex-class fleet carrier, was the first American aircraft carrier on duty off Korea. Later, the USS *Valley Forge* was joined by three sister ships as part of Task Force 77. (US National Archives)

used by the Marine Air Wing. The AD Skyraider was the workhorse of the US navy's attack aircraft. Operating from a carrier, it could carry a 7,500lb (3,400kg) payload. The Korean War was the first conflict where jets took off from aircraft carriers. F-9F Panther jet aircraft served in the dual role of fighter and strike aircraft. Unfortunately, its straight wings placed it at a disadvantage against the fast and maneuverable MiG-15.

A US navy Sikorsky HO35-1 helicopter. Helicopters made their first appearance in war in Korea. They proved their usefulness as a means of light transport and frequently engaged in search and rescue and medical evacuation missions. (US National Archives)

This Panther is conducting an interdiction strike against a small highway bridge. The pilot has already dropped one bomb and is in the process of dropping another. The smoke before the Panther's left wing is from a rocket that he has just launched. (US Naval Institute)

Patrolling, raiding, and digging

After November 1951, operations on the front settled into static warfare. Corporal Martin Russ served in the 1st US Marine Division in the last year of the war. His experiences are indicative of the life of a front-line soldier during the period of static warfare in the Korean War. Russ joined the Marines after completing his undergraduate education at St Laurence College. He was a member of Able Company, 1st Marine Regiment. During his time in Korea, he kept a daily journal of his experiences. It was later published as a book, *The Last Parallel*.

As a corporal, Russ was a non-commissioned officer. He carried a Browning automatic rifle (BAR), a 20 lb light machine-gun that provided rapid and long-range fire. Most infantry carried the semi-automatic

M-1 Garand Rifle. Another valuable item in Russ's kit was his armored flak vest. The flak vest made its first appearance in Korea. It contained fiberglass or nylon padding that reduced the impact of shell fragments but could not stop a bullet. By 1953, the vest had become a standard piece of personal equipment.

As static warfare set in, the Eighth Army front line began to resemble the Western Front of the First World War. The front line consisted of a Main Line of Resistance (MLR)

This Marine is removing a piece of shrapnel from his armored flak vest. It is probably exactly the same kind of vest that Corporal Martin Russ wore during his time on the front line. The vest consisted of fiberglass plates woven together. (Defence Department)

and a line of outposts. The MLR was a string of mutually supporting strongpoints, constructed to absorb and stop any enemy blow. Outposts were forward of the MLR within No Man's Land. They served to detect and slow an enemy advance. Bunkers, several aprons of barbed wire, and minefields protected most defensive positions. Bunkers were largely underground, with a roof of thick logs and sandbags to protect against artillery and mortar hits. Underground passageways often interconnected several bunkers. Each outpost and various points in No Man's Land were pinpointed so that mortars and artillery could deliver quick and accurate fire. Generally around a half mile (0.8km) wide, No Man's Land became familiar territory for both sides. In Russ's sector, it was littered with empty ration cans, discarded weapons, minefields, patrol paths, a burnt-out tank, downed Corsairs, and dead men.

Russ's platoon occupied an outpost, New Bunker Hill, for 16 days in March 1953. He defended a listening post within the front-line trench with one other man. There was a bunker directly behind his position and barbed wire in front of it. Further to the rear, there was

another bunker for sleeping. During the night, Chinese snipers observed and intermittently fired on New Bunker Hill. Russ always had to keep his head down and sleep curled up.

Patrols into No Man's Land were conducted both day and night. The object of a patrol was generally reconnaissance or combat. A reconnaissance patrol observed and kept contact with the enemy, reporting on unit identification, headquarters, locations, and the layout of his forward defenses. Combat patrols sought to fight the enemy, usually through staging an ambush or probing a Communist outpost. Patrols varied in size from a mere fire team to an entire platoon. Most front-line UNC companies conducted one patrol per night. Raids were conducted in platoon to battalion strength. They were mounted in order to seize a small outpost, capture prisoners, or simply harass the enemy.

An M-26 Pershing tank fires in support of the 24th US Division in January 1952. The Pershing was the only American tank that could stand up to a T-34. To provide the infantry with direct fire support, tanks were often positioned in fortified emplacements within the MLR. (The Tank Museum, Bovington)

Russ became adept at patrolling. He learned how to move stealthily and guide a patrol as a point-man. The Chinese frequently fired upon these patrols with mortars and machine-guns and, on a number of occasions, Russ engaged in actual firefights. In the dark, the enemy was rarely seen and aiming consisted of firing as much ammunition as possible in the general direction of the enemy's muzzle flashes. In April 1953, Russ became an acting squad leader and began leading more patrols.

For many UNC units, patrolling and raids proved burdensome. Raiding enemy outposts and capturing prisoners resulted in hard-fought battles and heavy casualties. Russ recorded that one proposed raid to capture a prisoner required 50 men, all of the regimental artillery and mortars, three tanks, two flame-throwing tanks, and a flight of Corsairs. Russ was very sceptical about American estimates of Chinese casualties from raids and patrols. He wrote of one particular estimate:

We scoffed at the estimate of Chinese casualties. From the little experience I've had in raids and from the stories I've heard of other raids, I'll bet the Chinese suffered half the number of casualties that we had. When we raid the Chinese, we get clobbered. When the Chinese raid the marines, they get clobbered worse. But they are a bit more intelligent about it; they don't make raids very often.

Nevertheless, formations that did not control No Man's Land, unlike the Marine or the Commonwealth Divisions, suffered heavy casualties and lost terrain to Communist surprise attacks.

Shortly before the end of the war, Russ was temporarily sent to Fox Company. Able Company was about to relieve them and Russ was to familiarize himself with Fox Company's positions and No Man's Land in that area. On his second night with Fox Company, Russ joined a 30-man combat patrol sent out to assault an enemy outpost. As the column approached the objective, the point-man discovered a trip wire across the path. The lieutenant followed the trip wire into a clump of bushes. Then, a burst of fire brought him down. The patrol had walked into a Chinese ambush. Russ described the following moments:

A tremendous volume of fire, coming from our right front, at a distance varying from twenty to fifty yards. These were the first muzzle blasts I noticed . . . Fire of equal intensity came from our left but at a greater distance. The ambush had been deployed in an inverted V formation and the fire from its apex was obviously the most deadly.

Nine of the first 10 Marines in the column were hit. A staff sergeant died in hand-to-hand combat trying to rescue the lieutenant, who was captured. Further back, after overcoming his surprise, Russ began to return fire with the BAR, along with the remaining members of the patrol. The firefight lasted for less than five minutes. Once the Marines had suppressed the Chinese fire, they aggressively began to withdraw.

The Chinese were still trying to surround the patrol and the Marines had to fight their way out. Moving back down the path, Russ spotted two Chinese approaching two prone Marines in a ditch less than 50 feet (15m) away. Later, Russ wrote what happened as the Chinese tried to drag one of the Marines away:

I was mesmerized ... It's taken me a month to even think about writing a description ... The BAR was not in firing position; it was necessary to bring it up from my side. I did this quickly, planting both elbows on the ground with an audible thud. I squeezed off an unnecessarily long burst before the Chinese could react. The muzzle blast was blinding ... When my eyes became again accustomed to the dark, I saw that one of the Chinese lay crumpled up near the edge of the paddy. The other was nowhere in sight. The Marine had been dragged only a few feet and ankles protruded from the first level or step of the paddy. At this moment – as I took notice of these things – I was fired upon from that area in which the two Chinese had appeared … I heaved grenades in that direction. After the explosions I could still hear people moving around in the paddy. Someone fell noisily into a puddle off to the left.

Of the two prone Marines, one was a corpsman (medic) playing dead and the other was unconscious. Russ and the corpsman lifted the unconscious Marine and withdrew to friendly lines. Six Marines were killed, 14 were wounded, and one was captured in the ambush. Chinese casualties were impossible to estimate in the confusion and uncertainty of night fighting.

Russ safely returned to the USA at the end of the war. In his last month in Korea, he was promoted to sergeant, a job whose duties he had been performing for some time as acting squad leader. He also earned a Purple Heart. Tiny splinters from a grenade and barbed wire had injured him during a combat patrol in May. He went on to write several books on Marines in combat in the Second World War, Korea, and Vietnam.

Members of 3 RAR out on patrol. Australian and British infantry were adept at
patrolling. Regular and aggressive patrols kept the Chinese bottled up on their side
of No Man's Land. (Imperial War Museum)

The domestic and international impact

One of the remarkable characteristics of the Korean War was its significance to events outside of the Korean peninsula. The conflict altered the domestic politics, economics, and security of regions far removed from the actual fighting.

Prisoners of war

By May 1952, the cease-fire delegations had reached an agreement on Item Three (cease-fire supervisory arrangements) through the establishment of a Neutral Nations Supervisory Commission and a Military Armistice Commission. Item Four (the exchange of prisoners of war), however, proved intractable. This issue typified the ideological conflict between democracy and Communism. In January 1952, Acheson and Truman decided to demand voluntary repatriation. This meant that every prisoner would have the right to return to his home country or seek residence in a new country. For the USA, voluntary repatriation was an inalienable right of all peoples. For the Communists, the potential defection of over 100,000 North Korean and Chinese prisoners would contradict the supposed utopia of their ideology. Both sides believed that conceding on this one issue would have dire effects on the acceptance of democracy or Communism throughout the world. Consequently, neither side was willing to yield.

The situation worsened in early 1952 when pro-Communist prisoners began violently resisting UNC authority in the prison on Koje-do, off the southern coast of South Korea. On 7 May 1952, pro-Communist prisoners captured the prison commandant, Brigadier-General Frank Dodd. China and North Korea

exploited the disorder to show that most prisoners indeed wanted to be repatriated and that the UNC demand for voluntary repatriation was unfounded. The crisis did not end until June 1952 when Brigadier-General Haydon Boatner, with considerable bloodshed, brought the situation under control.

American domestic politics

Within the USA, there was widespread apathy to the Korean War. Americans were particularly uneasy with the concept of limited war. The frequent reference to the war by government officials and the media as a 'police-action' seemed like a cynical understatement when Americans were dying in major battles. The phrase 'Why die for a tie?' was frequently used by opponents of limited war. Opposition to the war was fuelled by the Republican Congress, which sought to undermine the Truman administration. The strategy of limited war was presented as yet another example of the administration's appeasement of Communism.

The climax of the domestic American debate over limited war was sparked by MacArthur's dismissal. The American public and Congress were outraged. A Gallup Poll gave Truman a mere 29 percent approval rating. MacArthur returned to the USA as a hero. On 19 April 1951, he spoke before the US Congress and attacked the concept of limited war as immoral. He said: 'once war is forced upon us, there is no other alternative than to apply every available means to bring it to a swift end . . . War's very object is victory, not prolonged indecision. In war there is no substitute for victory.' He ended the speech with the famous line: 'Old Soldiers

Communist prisoners in a compound at Koje-do holding a demonstration against voluntary repatriation. Actions like this undermined the UNC stand for voluntary repatriation in the eyes of the world. (Defence Department)

never die, they just fade away.' Several Senators and Congressmen were in tears.

Looking for further political gains, the Republican Senate opened the MacArthur Hearings in June 1951 as a means of indicting the Truman administration for the dismissal of MacArthur and the strategy of limited war. MacArthur again appeared before the Congress and attacked the concept of limited war. Then, Acheson, Marshall, and Bradley testified in defense of the Truman administration's actions. Bradley convincingly stated that MacArthur had disobeyed a presidential order to clear his public statements with Washington. In doing so, he had promulgated an American foreign policy to the world that contradicted Truman's actual policy. Bradley also argued

that fighting a total war with the PRC would involve a major diversion of American resources from confronting the Soviet Union in more critical areas. He said: 'Red China is not the powerful nation seeking to dominate the world. Frankly, in the opinion of the Joint Chiefs of Staff, this strategy would involve us in the wrong war, at the wrong place, at the wrong time, and with the wrong enemy.' Partly because of Bradley's testimony, the MacArthur Hearings failed to discredit the Truman administration's handling of the war.

After the MacArthur Hearings, popular opposition to the war died down, but it never faded away. The country grew tired of interminable peace negotiations and the stalemate on the battlefield. Consequently, there was broad support for Eisenhower's campaign promises in 1952 to 'Go to Korea' and bring a swift end to the war. This domestic attitude provided impetus for Eisenhower's preparations to escalate the war in 1953. Nevertheless, there was always a substantial percentage of the population in favor of peace talks and a compromise solution to the war. Indeed, many Americans disliked the indecisive way the war was fought, yet approved of the cease-fire talks and the values of compromise and moderation they embodied.

Geostrategic implications

One of the most important effects of the Korean War was the degree to which it mobilized the West against Soviet expansionism. By signaling that the Communists truly had aggressive intentions, the Korean War led to a massive mobilization of Western resources for war and gave the Cold War its notorious complexion of two armed camps irreconcilably opposed to one another.

The outbreak of the Korean War caused the USA to undergo a massive rearmament program. The attack confirmed the assumptions about Communist aggression made in NSC 68. Accordingly, NSC 68's prescriptions were rapidly implemented. As early as July 1950, Truman requested that Congress add $10 billion to the $14 billion US defense budget, remove the manpower limit on the size of the American armed forces, and provide greater military aid to friendly countries. In September, Congress approved. Military expansion continued throughout the Korean War. For example, by July 1951, the USA's military strength had doubled and the defense budget for 1952 was four times that of 1949.

The defense of Western Europe was also bolstered. The West feared that the Korean War was merely a prelude to a Soviet invasion of Western Europe. In 1950, only 14 weak divisions were assigned to NATO and there was no unified command structure. No American divisions were even deployed in Europe. Shortly after the outbreak of the Korean War, the USA put forward a 'one package' proposal for an increase in American divisions assigned to NATO, a build-up of the French and British

armed forces, German rearmament, and an integrated and centralized command structure. In the first three months of the war, France and Britain took significant steps to build their armed forces. By 1953, 15 well-armed divisions, including six American, were deployed in West Germany as part of NATO. The percentage of gross domestic product spent on military expenditures increased from an average of 5.5 percent to 12 percent for NATO countries. The Supreme Headquarters Allied Powers Europe was established to integrate planning and to command NATO forces in the event of war. Finally, serious deliberations began on German rearmament.

The Korean War also led the USA to recognize east Asia as an area of vital strategic importance. Prompted by the urgency of the Korean War, on 8 September 1951 the USA and Japan signed a peace treaty, normalizing their post-Second World War relations. A military alliance, the Japan–US Security Treaty, was established shortly thereafter, in 1952. Partly to offset fears of a resurgence of Japanese militarism and partly to oppose Communism, the USA signed security pacts with Australia, New Zealand, and the Philippines in the same month. In addition to these moves, the USA increased its support of France in its war against Ho Chi Minh in Indochina. At the conclusion of the war the US also signed a mutual security treaty with South Korea.

The economic situation in the PRC and North Korea

The Communists were feeling the strain of extended warfare by 1953. China's and North Korea's poorly industrialized economic systems were not suited to sustaining high-intensity modern warfare. For the PRC, the Korean War had come too soon after the Second World War and the Chinese Civil War. Mao's plans for a gradual and peaceful transition to socialism – including continued trade with the West – had to be set aside in order to mobilize the economy in support of the war effort.

Socialism was rapidly instituted in the PRC along Soviet, instead of Chinese, models of economic development, and forced economic activity caused inflation to run rampant. In 1951, 50 percent of the PRC's revenues were dedicated to the war, but despite heavy taxation, the Chinese government lacked the revenues to pay for its expenditures and the PRC was burdened with a hefty debt. The CCP was also concerned about the possibility of internal dissension. After decades of conflict, the Chinese people were becoming increasingly war weary. These economic and political concerns compelled Mao to end the war. In the fall of 1952, Zhou met with Stalin in Moscow. Zhou sought to conclude an armistice if the UNC made some minor concessions at the negotiating table. But Stalin opposed the idea because he did not want to end the drain on US military resources.

North Korea was in even worse condition than China. The economy was in ruins and the country was wracked by food shortages. The air campaign had destroyed the country's industrial facilities and caused heavy

bomb damage to every major city. Towns and villages, often the location of supply depots, were repeatedly targeted for UNC air strikes. Most North Korean civilians fled to the countryside to escape the bombing. Major-General William Dean, a prisoner of war, reported that by 1952 the majority of the towns he observed were 'rubble or snowy open spaces.' And most North Koreans he met had lost a relative in an air strike. In the summer of 1952, Kim pleaded with Stalin to implement a more decisive strategy in order to reduce North Korea's hardship. Thus, the cumulative costs of war were driving both North Korea and the PRC to seek to end the fighting. Only Stalin's obstinacy and determination to wear down the West perpetuated the conflict.

The devastated industrial area of Chongjin in North Korea. North Korea's industry was almost entirely destroyed in the course of the war. In the era before smart weapons, collateral bomb damage was inescapably high. Significant portions of all of the major cities and towns in North Korea were reduced to rubble. (Defence Department)

Kyonshill Kang

As noted previously, Korea was torn apart during the three years of the Korean War. The war might have been a limited endeavor for the USA and the Soviet Union, but it was nothing less than a total war for the Korean people. As a young girl, Kyonshill Kang went through the ebb and flow of Communist and UNC offensives in South Korea. She described her experiences in her book, *Home was the Land of Morning Calm: A Saga of a Korean-American Family*. Her family was originally from Tanchon, a city near the east coast of North Korea. The increasing Communist control of North Korea after 1945 caused her family to move to South Korea in 1946. In fact, her grandmother crossed the border five times in order to guide all of the family members into South Korea. Living in Seoul, her father, a teacher, attained a respectable position and earned a reasonable standard of living. Kang remembered hearing Rhee speak once. Most Koreans were impressed with him because he was the first Korean to have earned a PhD in the USA.

A Korean family treks southward during the Fifth Phase Offensive. The mobile warfare of the first year of the war resulted in a huge number of refugees. (US Army)

Kang's family first heard about the war on 26 June 1950 through the radio. Rhee made a subsequent radio broadcast that it was safe to remain in Seoul. Although her grandmother and mother (her father was in the USA as a Fulbright scholar) were worried about the invasion, they were reassured by Rhee's announcement. Six days later, they learned that Rhee and most of his government had actually fled Seoul immediately after the radio broadcast. This caused the population of Seoul to panic. Nevertheless, by that time, Kang's grandmother had decided that it was wisest to stay in Seoul. At night, they could hear artillery fire. Meanwhile, thousands fled south on foot or by train. The roads were clogged with refugees. By the end of July,

25,000 Koreans per day were crossing UNC lines. Many died during the journey.

The North Koreans tried to reconstruct South Korea into a Communist state. They instituted people's committees and created Communist socio-political organizations. Land reform was implemented and tenant farming was abolished. Leftist South Koreans assisted the North Koreans. Many members of the National Assembly were neither as cowardly nor as wise as Rhee to flee Seoul. Several were executed by the North Koreans for their political beliefs. As David Rees related in *Korea: The Limited War*, one captured Communist guerrilla diary read: 'Apprehended twelve men; National Assembly members, police

sergeants, and Myon [a town] leaders. Killed four of them at the scene, and the remaining eight were shot after investigation by the People's court.' The North Koreans committed similar atrocities throughout South Korea against Christians, rightists, and anyone else suspected of opposing Communism.

When the North Korean soldiers entered Kang's neighborhood, many Communist sympathizers spontaneously appeared. They formed block committees and observed the activities of everyone in the neighborhood. Every household was required to display pictures of Kim and Stalin. For a time, young high school girls who supported the North Koreans boarded with Kang's family and extolled the virtues of Communism to her. The neighborhood even had to learn a Communist song:

> *Marks of blood on every ridge of the Jangbaek*
> *Marks of blood on every ridge of Amnol*
> *Still now over the blooming free Korea*
> *Those sacred marks shed brilliant rays*
> *O dear is the name, our beloved general*
> *O glorious is the name, General Kim Il Sung.*

North Korean soldiers and South Korean civilians dance in Seoul following its occupation in the summer of 1950. Many South Koreans were apathetic towards the North Korean invasion, but some actively supported it. (US National Archives)

All adult males were conscripted for manual labor, serving as porters and hauling ammunition for the NKPA. Women were eventually recruited as well. To avoid their conscription, Kang's family hid her uncle and a family friend, 'Teacher' Song, in small uncomfortable spaces in the house. The men remained there, only emerging to relieve themselves, until August. Kang was given the duty of signaling whenever any possible informants entered the neighborhood. As the weeks drifted into months, food supplies became scarce. The family hid their rice so that the Communists could not requisition it.

The family witnessed frequent American air strikes. They took shelter in the basement whenever the shiny fuselage of a B-29 was spotted. Air raids usually lasted over an hour. Although most of the American targets were supply depots, once a school was mistakenly bombed where civilians were taking refuge; several died. In September 1950, Kang's family heard the artillery of the approaching Marines. Kang remembered the arrival of 'pink-faced' Americans and the widespread and newfound optimism about the course of the war. This was quickly shattered, though, by the Chinese intervention. Her uncle and 'Teacher' Song were respectively conscripted into the ROK army and manual labor. When the Communists approached Seoul again in January 1951, the family fled to Pusan through Taejon, leaving behind most of their possessions. Kang and her mother traveled on the rooftop of a train against the bitterly cold winter wind. Kang's mother kept her awake throughout the trip to prevent hypothermia.

In Pusan, the family entered a packed refugee camp in Pusan. Thin partitions of sheets and rags separated each family's living space. Life was very difficult. Pusan was crowded and dirty, and there were frequent power outages and water shortages. Kang remembered standing in line for hours for water. Many Korean women became prostitutes to earn money, which only gained them the condemnation of the rest of the Korean community. Children jeered at any Korean woman walking with an American soldier as a 'Western whore.'

Many Koreans believed that Americans and other white UNC troops viewed them as inferior. While still in Korea, Kang's father had felt that Americans looked down upon Koreans. The slang name for all Koreans, 'gook,' certainly was not endearing. Of greater infamy is the massacre of South Korean civilians at No Gun Ri by the 7th US Cavalry Regiment in July 1950. Units of the regiment were retreating from the North Koreans and found their path underneath a bridge blocked by refugees. Fearing that North Korean soldiers might be hiding among the crowd, the Americans opened fire, killing perhaps 100 South Korean civilians. However, racism and brutality to civilians were by no means universal. Many Americans were impressed by the hardships endured by the Korean people as well as the courage of their soldiers.

South Koreans generally did not support the UNC strategy of fighting a limited war. They wanted Korea unified. Even before the war, Kang remembered singing songs about unification. Kang's father was resentful that the superpowers had arbitrarily divided the peninsula. He despised Roosevelt for abandoning democracy in Korea. Given his plans to unify Korea, most South Koreans admired MacArthur. They considered many of MacArthur's bad qualities – his arrogance, authoritarianism, and vanity – necessary in a strong leader. Kang's family was shocked when he was dismissed.

Rhee's government was authoritarian and despite Rhee's example, corruption existed. His police forces executed and imprisoned hundreds of Communist collaborators. Rhee and the National Assembly were in constant conflict. The ROK President was chosen by the National Assembly, not directly elected by the people, among whom Rhee was more popular. Therefore, Rhee wanted the National Assembly to change the ROK constitution so that he would be elected directly. To effect this, Rhee declared martial law and imprisoned several members of the National Assembly in May 1952. The National Assembly conceded in July, after the domestic political stability of South Korea had been placed in question for months, and the principles for which the UN allies were fighting had been treated with contempt.

South Korea endured many more hardships before the war ended, such as rampant inflation and slow economic growth. For Kang's family, life eventually improved. They were given a room in Pusan outside of the refugee camp and Kang's resourceful grandmother began peddling goods. Kang herself attended a refugee school and learned new songs about UNC, instead of Communist, valor. In the summer of 1951, they discovered that her father was working in UNC general headquarters in Tokyo. In late 1952, the family left for Japan, and from there they would eventually move to the USA.

Closing moves

In the last nine months of the Korean War, the USA and the Chinese searched for political and military means to end the war. Heightened combat matched the final steps toward peace, as both sides tried to use military force to strengthen their respective bargaining positions.

New armies

One of the important outcomes of the Korean War was the modernization of the ROK army and the Chinese People's Volunteers. After 1951, the major events in the ground war involved battles between these two reformed armies. The South Korean army was very important to the USA in lessening the burden placed on American military resources. After the Fifth Phase Offensive, Van Fleet, who had been instrumental in rebuilding the Greek army after the Second World War, was determined to modernize the ROK army. The Eighth Army initiated a program, 'Concentrated Training for the ROK Army,' to guide modernization. A Field Training Command used American officers and NCOs to train each ROK division in operations from individual to company level. Selected ROK officers went to infantry or artillery school in the USA. Additionally, a staff school and a military academy were established in Korea. Meanwhile, the divisions were given proper levels of equipment. In January 1952, Van Fleet decided to rebuild the II ROK Corps and place it under the command of Major-General Paik Sun Yup. Unlike previous ROK corps, the new corps headquarters would have artillery, engineer, and quartermaster supporting units directly under its command. The II ROK Corps entered the line in April 1952 between the IX and X US Corps, a symbol of the new ROK army.

The CPV also underwent major reforms in 1952. The first half of 1952 was spent strengthening the front line, bringing forward reinforcements and new equipment, and indoctrinating tactical lessons. The Chinese extended and improved their fortifications from the front line to the waist of Korea. Several Communist armies were echeloned behind the front line and along the North Korean coasts. Concrete bunkers dotted the Communist positions. Giant tunnels, some 100 feet (30m) deep, interconnecting trenches, and fieldworks were constructed, to protect the soldiers from UNC firepower. Assault units used the tunnels to approach UNC outposts undetected. Logistics were also developed and improved. Over 180,000 rear servicemen were dedicated to supporting the Communist fighting units. Against these defenses, any major UNC offensive would now be extremely difficult.

Mao was still resolved to fight a protracted war, believing that the USA would cave in under prolonged attrition. But to do so, a method of fighting needed to be developed that would reduce Chinese casualties. In April 1952, Peng returned to Beijing to oversee the Central Military Commission (the PLA high command). Although Peng was still officially commander of the CPV, Deng Hua became the acting commander and Yang Dezhi, commander of the Nineteenth CPV Army Corps, was given charge of all combat operations. 'Active positional defense' became the new doctrine of the CPV. Any UNC advance would be immediately counterattacked with CPV reserves. Small attacks on enemy outposts would seize the initiative and destroy UNC units piecemeal in 'see-saw battles'. In the course of the continuing battles, the tactics of 'see-saw

Chinese soldiers conferring underground. The Communists built extensive underground fortifications along their MLR and back to the waist of Korea from the summer of 1951 until the end of the war. Large tunnels cut through their defensive positions. (Chinese National Army Museum)

battles' were modified in order to reduce casualties. Chinese infantry rarely made the kind of unsupported mass frontal assaults that had marked their earlier tactics. Rather, careful reconnaissance, combined-arms tactics, artillery preparation, and concentration of forces were emphasized. Army commanders were to be certain of success before launching an attack.

In early September 1952, Deng and Yang began a series of attacks against a salient held by the II ROK Corps, known as the Kumsong bulge. In October, the CPV

captured several outposts and briefly
penetrated the Eighth Army MLR. Once the
Chinese attacks lost momentum, Van Fleet
ordered the IX US Corps to launch a
counterattack, Operation Showdown, on
10 October. Given that this area had been
the focus of operations for the past month,
the Chinese were ready for the attack. For six
weeks, a major 'see-saw' battle persisted in an
area of less than three square miles
(7.75km²).

Deng was pleased with the opportunity to
destroy UNC manpower. The mountainous
area, laced with Communist fortifications,
was well suited for defense. Once more, the
South Koreans did most of the fighting.
Supported by American firepower, they drove
the Chinese into their tunnels during the
day. The Chinese would then counterattack
at night and regain their positions. One
position, Sniper Ridge, changed hands
14 times. Deng and Yang fed reinforcements
into the battle until they held all of the
important terrain. Given the heavy UNC
casualties and under pressure from Clark and
Collins, Van Fleet broke off Operation
Showdown on 28 November.

The battles of fall 1952 were the first
significant Communist successes since the
Second Phase Offensive. Van Fleet had
committed a major operational error in
submitting to this kind of slugfest. UNC
casualties were over 9,000. The CPV lost
11,500 men but could sustain these losses.
By emphasizing concentration, firepower,
and better infantry tactics, Deng and Yang
learned that they could wear down the UNC
without suffering exorbitant losses to their
own forces in the process.

Threats of escalation

Dwight Eisenhower was elected President of
the United States in November 1952. It was
widely believed that he would embrace a
decisive military strategy. However,
Eisenhower was actually very cautious. He
was wary of making any reckless moves that
might cause the Soviets to intervene.

Nevertheless, he and his administration were
firmly resolved to end the war quickly. By
signaling that the USA was willing to fight a
much bigger and more destructive war,
Eisenhower and Secretary of State John Foster
Dulles hoped to convince the Communists
that further fighting was not worthwhile.

The use of atomic weapons was a very
dangerous proposition. In the early 1950s, the
USA did not possess a large stock of atomic
bombs. A saturation bombing of the PRC or
even the Communist front line was out of the
question. Atomic weapons could only be used
to support an Eighth Army advance or destroy
certain military and industrial targets in
North Korea or the PRC. On the other hand,
the UNC was very vulnerable to atomic
attack. The huge supply base at Pusan and the
cities of Japan would be particularly lucrative
targets for the Communists. Escalating the
war conventionally was not an easy task
either. The UNC lacked the manpower and
materiel to launch a major ground offensive
against the strong Communist defenses. At
least six months would be required to build
the forces necessary for an offensive to the
waist of the peninsula.

In the fall of 1952, Clark began pressing for
escalated American military action. On
8 October, after weeks of deadlock, Clark
recessed negotiations indefinitely. He then
presented the JCS with a plan to compel the
Communists to agree to a cease-fire on
American terms. He wanted to blockade
China, bomb targets in north China and
Manchuria, and launch a ground offensive
to the Yalu. Clark requested that the JCS plan
to use nuclear weapons in the attack. The
JCS would not authorize the plan. When
Eisenhower visited Korea in late 1952 as
president-elect, Clark pressed for the plan's
implementation. Eisenhower also rejected it.
Nevertheless, when Eisenhower returned to
the USA, and later in his State of the Union
address, he hinted that he might escalate
the war.

As noted previously, by the end of 1952
both the Chinese and the North Koreans
were feeling the strain of war and looking for
a way out. However, Stalin had been refusing

to end the war. Predicting that a Third World War with the West was inevitable, he believed that compromise in Korea would damage Communist prestige and end the drain on Western resources that the war entailed. Stalin died on 5 March 1953. The new Soviet leadership wanted to pursue a less confrontational mode of competition with the USA. Thus, at Stalin's funeral, they were receptive to Zhou's proposal for compromising on a cease-fire in Korea. The Soviet leadership appreciated that the continued costs of war were too high and agreed that the stand on forcible repatriation should be abandoned.

Accordingly, on 28 March 1953, Zhou accepted a February proposal by Clark, dubbed 'Little Switch,' for an exchange of sick and wounded prisoners of war. Progress in negotiations followed. On 26 April, the six-month recess in negotiations finally ended. In early May, the Communists proposed a Neutral Nations Repatriation Commission. The commission would temporarily supervise the POWs in Korea after the armistice. Each side would be allowed to send representatives to convince their prisoners to return home. However, no prisoner would be repatriated against his wishes. Unfortunately, minor disagreements impeded the quick conclusion of negotiations, leading to a new round of heightened military activity.

Despite compromising at the negotiation table, Deng and Mao continued to pressure the UNC on the battlefield. This was partly a means of saving face while making concessions. More importantly, though, Deng and the other CPV generals seriously believed that the UNC would not come to terms unless they suffered unsustainable losses. The initial attacks focused on the ROK army in the east and American and Commonwealth forces in the west. But when Rhee opposed UNC compromises at Panmunjom, Deng and Yang refocused their attacks upon ROK formations.

On 10 June, the Chinese attacked the II ROK Corps around Kumsong. With heavy artillery support, the Chinese pressed forward 2 miles (3.2 km) and into the MLR by 14 June. The South Koreans fought back hard. They established blocking positions and moved reserves to the front. The onslaught continued until the first cease-fire was concluded on 16 June. The CPV had suffered 6,600 casualties while the South Koreans had lost 7,300 men. CPV commanders were convinced that this offensive brought the UNC to terms. Actually, American decision-makers were too focused on the possibility of escalating the war to be affected by this relatively minor defeat, especially as most of the casualties were South Koreans, not Americans.

While the Communists attacked on the ground, the USA and UNC intensified the air war. For the first time, Sabre squadrons were instructed to seek out and destroy the MiG-15s in MiG Alley, rather than merely to ward off their attacks. The object was to destroy the enemy aircraft faster than new pilots could be trained for combat. Sabre sorties doubled in the last months of the war. Unfortunately for the Chinese, the Soviets decided to withdraw their air divisions in late April. The Chinese were decimated. The Sabres shot down over 150 MiG-15s in May, June, and July 1953; by far the greatest Communist monthly losses of the war.

Additionally, Clark targeted 20 dams in North Korea for destruction. Doing so would flood North Korea's rice fields and inhibit the country from feeding itself. In the past, such agricultural targets had been avoided because of humanitarian concerns and the risk of escalation. Starting on 13 May, FEAF fighter-bombers struck five dams, including Toksan, near Pyongyang. The rice fields were flooded and 70 nearby villages were allegedly submerged. The North Koreans scrambled to repair the damage and enact preventive measures as the strikes continued. Bombing was also renewed against the North Korean hydroelectric plants, some of which had been repaired.

In March 1953, the JCS and the NSC, believing that the Communists were not feeling sufficient military pressure, began discussing ending restrictions on all operations. Specifically, they studied NSC

A South Korean mortar team on Capitol Hill. Capitol Hill was one of the several terrain features fiercely fought over during the 'see-saw' battles of fall 1952. Although it was eventually lost, the South Koreans defended the hill staunchly and inflicted numerous casualties on the Chinese. (Defence Department)

147, which outlined options for an advance to the waist of Korea, bombing air bases in Manchuria, and the use of atomic weapons. Bradley and Eisenhower worried that the last option could dramatically escalate the conflict and cause Soviet retaliation. After much deliberation, on 19 May, the JCS endorsed the implementation of options within NSC 147, including the use of atomic weapons, if there was no progress in negotiations in the next months. Eisenhower approved NSC 147 as a rough guide for

strategy if escalation became necessary.

Following the endorsement of NSC 147, American leaders issued a series of nuclear threats. First, on 21 May, Dulles told Indian Prime Minister Jawaharlal Nehru that the USA would expand military action if the current round of talks failed. Dulles expected that his statement would be relayed to the Chinese. Second, on 27 May, Clark sent Kim and Peng a letter stating that negotiations had reached their final stage. Third, on 3 June, Ambassador Charles Bohlen in Moscow told Soviet Foreign Minister Vyacheslav Molotov that the failure of armistice talks would create a situation that the USA hoped to avoid. All of these statements were meant to convey American intent to escalate the war, and possibly use atomic weapons, if the

Communists did not concede soon in negotiations.

The UNC delegation presented their 'final position' on 25 May 1953. It accepted the Communist proposal for a Neutral Nations Repatriation Commission and made a number of concessions on the details of an agreement. If the Communists did not accept the 'final

South Koreans demonstrating against an armistice in Seoul. Most South Koreans supported President Rhee's stance that an armistice should not be concluded until North Korea was liberated. (Defence Department)

position,' Clark was authorized to end negotiations and escalate military action, including implementing his offensive plan from October 1952. In the event, the Communists accepted the final position. This allowed a cease-fire agreement to be concluded to take effect on 27 July. On that day the 15 nations supporting South Korea signed the China Warning Statement, which threatened that renewed aggression would make them return to hostilities, which probably could not be confined within the borders of Korea.

South Korean President Syngman Rhee speaking with US Ambassador Muccio. In June 1953, Rhee unilaterally released 25,000 North Korean prisoners of war because of his opposition to the armistice accords. (Defence Department)

Rhee vociferously opposed the armistice. He wanted Korea unified and all Chinese forces withdrawn from Korea. Koreans filled the streets of Seoul and other cities throughout South Korea to demonstrate against an armistice. The climactic event occurred on 18 June when Rhee unilaterally released 25,000 North Korean prisoners of war. Clark and Eisenhower were surprised and angered. Urgent negotiations ensued between Rhee and Clark. Clark finally secured Rhee's acceptance of the armistice agreement by promising that the USA would sign a security treaty with the ROK and continue to build the ROK armed forces after the war.

Not surprisingly, the Communists were outraged by Rhee's intransigent act. Mao

The Kumsong bulge and the final armistice line, 27 July 1953

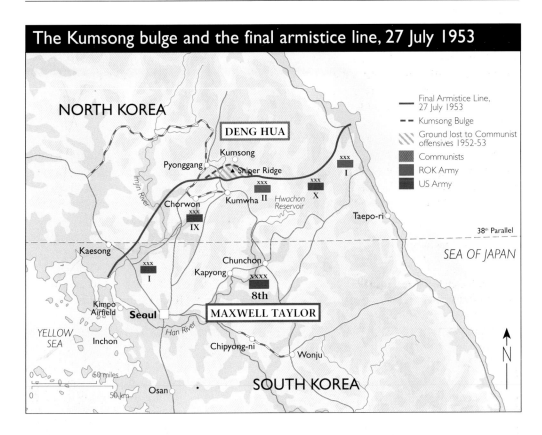

From September 1952 to July 1953, a series of 'see-saw battles' were fought for the Kumsong bulge. By the end of the war, the Chinese had captured most of it.

ordered another offensive in order to punish Rhee and demonstrate Chinese resolve. On 13 July, five CPV armies (150,000 men) again attacked the II ROK Corps defending the Kumsong bulge. Exploiting tactical surprise, darkness, and overwhelming numbers, the Chinese broke through the MLR along 21 miles (34km) of front. The South Koreans were forced to withdraw 19 miles (31km) to avoid encirclement. Nevertheless, the South Koreans were fighting hard and not panicking. Once again, the new ROK army proved its resilience. Morale was high and units were not dissolving. After 16 July, ROK formations began to counterattack and even pushed the Communists back 5 miles (8km). But the Chinese were not seeking to scrap the armistice agreement. After attaining success on the battlefield,

the Communists signed a second cease-fire on 27 July 1953.

Conventional wisdom claims that Eisenhower's nuclear threats compelled the Communists to compromise and end the Korean War. There is actually little evidence to support that claim. Eisenhower's nuclear threats were important, in that they signaled that the USA countenanced continued and heightened warfare. But the Communists were motivated to compromise primarily by the exhaustion of nearly three years of war. The cumulative loss of manpower, destruction of industry, and military expenditures were a heavy burden. By early 1953, continuing to bear this burden was not worthwhile, even though the CPV was a more efficient fighting force than ever before. The key event that facilitated the Communist decision to compromise was Stalin's death. The institution of more moderate leadership in Moscow enabled the PRC and North Korea to make the concessions necessary to reach an armistice.

The significance of the Korean War in the history of warfare

In spite of its limited nature, the Korean War was tremendously destructive. Korea's industrial base was wiped out. Four million Koreans, 10 percent of the population, were rendered casualties and five million became refugees. The North Korean armed forces lost approximately 600,000 men in the fighting, in addition to two million civilian casualties. The Chinese suffered an estimated one million casualties. Losses to the ROK armed forces are estimated at 70,000 killed, 150,000 wounded, and 80,000 captured (the majority of whom died from starvation or mistreatment). One million South Korean civilians were killed or injured. The USA lost 33,600 men killed and 103,200 wounded.

The Korean peninsula was divided along the line of contact at the end of the war and remains so to this day. A political conference called for in the armistice agreement was held in Geneva in 1954, but the two sides' demands were too far apart to permit any compromise. The peninsula became a microcosm of the Cold War itself. Heavily armed, North and South Korea faced each other across the demilitarized zone. But, other than desultory skirmishing, a second war has not broken out.

South Korea emerged from the war militarily secure but domestically unstable. The ROK armed forces had grown to number 600,000 men. They could hold their own against the North Koreans and, to a lesser extent, the Chinese. Following his unilateral release of North Korean POWs, Rhee had secured from the USA a mutual defense treaty, long-term economic aid, and assistance in expanding the ROK armed forces. Additionally, the Eighth Army remained in South Korea throughout the Cold War. The ROK was now an important bulwark against Communist expansionism in east Asia. It would be one of the few nations to provide a sizable military contribution to the American war effort in Vietnam. However, South Korea would not experience substantial economic growth until the 1960s. The constant threat of war led Rhee toward greater authoritarianism and high levels of military spending, which detracted from economic development. The political context of South Korea was marked by authoritarian governments and intermittent student protests. Rhee himself was overthrown in a *coup d'état* in 1961.

North Korea remained a potent military power after the war. Close ties were maintained with the Soviet Union and the PRC. Indeed, North Korea became intensely Communist. The re-indoctrination of Communism was necessary to mobilize sufficient resources for economic reconstruction. The effort was largely successful, and the North Korean economy was rebuilt by the late 1950s. Politically, the defeats of the Korean War undercut Kim Il Sung's leadership position. In order to stay in power, he executed a number of his opponents. He then built a cult of personality around the myth that North Korea had won the Korean War. Kim ultimately survived the Cold War, and North Korea remains a Communist state to this day under his son's leadership.

The Korean War is often considered a draw or even a defeat for the UNC. The Soviet Union and the PRC had achieved their minimal goal of defending their positions in east Asia. The two countries remained powerful obstacles to American hegemony in the area. The independence of North Korea had been preserved. However, this reasoning assumes that the lack of total victory was a defeat. In fact, the Korean War was an unmistakable victory for the UNC.

First, the important UNC demands were met in negotiations. Concessions were only made on minor points. The line of contact, not the 38th Parallel, became the border between North and South Korea, and voluntary repatriation was enforced. Second, in the course of military operations, the Communists suffered far greater manpower and economic losses than the UNC. For the PRC and North Korea, the opportunity cost of these lost resources for internal development was great. Third, the West halted the first major Communist attempt at overt aggression. Without delving into a counterfactual, it is reasonable to assume that if South Korea had not been successfully defended, China and the Soviet Union would have continued with a more overtly aggressive foreign policy against the West. Instead, for the remainder of the Cold War, they resorted to guerrilla warfare as the primary means of expanding their influence.

There were no truly decisive battles in the Korean War. Success for the Communists or the UNC ultimately depended on their ability to sustain protracted warfare through a combination of economic strength and military efficiency. The Communists proved less able to do so. Despite their numerical superiority, the Communists needed to break the military ascendancy of the UNC before the weakness of their economic systems made continued warfare unacceptably expensive. Instead, the clumsy Communist tactics in the first year of the war and Ridgway's generalship crippled their war effort. Deng Hua and Yang Dezhi did a remarkable job reforming the CPV in 1952. But by the time these reforms took effect, the Chinese could no longer shoulder the costs of war.

After overcoming the initial Chinese intervention, the UNC became an exceptionally efficient military force. The UNC mounted offensives without sustaining heavy casualties; repeatedly halted Communist attacks; conducted air strikes throughout North Korea; and controlled the seas surrounding the peninsula. Technological superiority, abundance of firepower, a core of experienced soldiers, and innovating commanders engendered military efficiency. Moreover, the economic strength of the USA meant that the UNC could fight the war virtually indefinitely. China's economy, on the other hand, had never recovered from the Chinese Civil War or the Second World War. As the Korean War dragged on, the need for internal economic development and an end to the burden of military expenditure created an impetus for compromise. For the Soviet Union, the heavy costs of financing and supplying a major regional war were not worth the marginal reward of enforcing the Communist bargaining position in negotiations. Hence, by 1953, the Communists preferred to compromise rather than overburden their economies with an interminable war.

The Korean War had wide implications for the entire international system. First, as technically a United Nations action, the Korean War was pivotal in the development of that organization. Second, in the area of military strategy, Korea was significant as the first limited war. Hard practical experience in the Korean War had raised major questions regarding the usability of nuclear weapons. Third, and most importantly, the war affected the balance of power between the two superpowers.

It was in Korea that the UN first authorized the use of force in the name of collective security. Unfortunately, the Korean War showed that, in reality, the UN was not a guarantor of collective security. UN action was a fluke resulting from Soviet absence in the Security Council. The UN was not acting out the will of the entire international community, but that of the West. Later in the Cold War, UN action in support of collective security was usually impossible because of opposition from either the USA or the Soviet Union, depending on whose sphere of influence the UN was considering intervening in. Nevertheless, several important diplomatic initiatives originated in the UN, including the first cease-fire resolution in December

1950 and Jacob Malik's proposal for negotiations in June 1951. The 'Uniting for Peace' procedure was also created in the Korean War. It would be used again in the Cold War, most notably as a means for the USA to punish the British and French during the Suez Canal Crisis. Most importantly, the fact that the Korean War was heavily debated in the UN by all member states validated the UN's role as the legitimate mediator of international conflicts and a forum for diplomacy.

Regarding military strategy, the Korean War was the first illustration of the new context of warfare that emerged in the Cold War. The former aim of warfare, the total annihilation of an opponent, was excessively dangerous. The dramatic victories of the North Korean blitzkrieg, the Inchon landing, and the Second Phase Offensive caused a rapid escalation of the Korean War that brought each combatant to the brink of world war. A limited aim was now the goal of most wars. In Korea, and frequently thereafter, a limited aim embodied seeking minor political gains through a negotiated resolution of the war. Military operations were carefully restrained in order to reduce the risk of escalation. Similar restrictions on military operations would reappear in subsequent wars, such as Vietnam, the Arab–Israeli Wars, and the Indo-Pakistani Wars. The methods of warfare implemented under these restrictions in the Korean War – attrition, air power, and nuclear threats – were the first adaptations to limited war. Consequently, the Korean War was the formative experience in the strategic thought and operational doctrines developed during the Cold War.

Attrition was the first method of warfare that the UNC applied to fighting a limited war. Ridgway found that gradual and careful attrition could defeat the Communists on the battlefield and enforce the UNC bargaining position yet not escalate the conflict. The significance of attrition was underlined when Peng Dehuai and Deng Hua adopted it as the operational doctrine of the CPV. However, because of its

protracted nature, attrition on the ground entailed a steady flow of casualties for both the UNC and the Communists. Indeed, after 1953, the Eisenhower administration forswore the use of conventional force largely because of the costs of attrition in Korea. Nevertheless, attrition would be applied as a strategy in many later conflicts in the Cold War – not always successfully – such as Vietnam, the Egyptian–Israeli War of Attrition, and the Iran–Iraq War.

The use of air power was less effective as a means of fighting a limited war. It could not inflict the damage necessary to make the Communists crack. Nevertheless, it remained a preferred, if often overrated, means of applying force after Korea. In the US air force, the perceived success of the air campaign was used to confirm the decisiveness of air power in modern warfare. Strategic air campaigns that were very similar to Operation Strangle and the sustained air pressure strategy were implemented in Vietnam, the 1991 Gulf War, and the 1999 conflict in Kosovo. Although rarely decisive, the allure of a painless and quick victory makes air power the West's principal means of waging war to this day.

Eisenhower's nuclear threats represented the final new method of warfare implemented in Korea. As noted above, while the nuclear threats signaled that the USA was resolved to fight a heightened war if necessary, they probably had only a marginal effect on the Communist decision to compromise. Historically, the nuclear threats were a part of the development of deterrence strategy, which dominated strategic discourse in the Cold War. In 1954, Eisenhower and Dulles instituted the New Look doctrine, hoping to repeat the supposed success of their nuclear threats at the end of the Korean War. The New Look threatened that Communist aggression anywhere in the world would be the subject of a devastating American nuclear strike. It was believed that this threat of massive retaliation would deter future Communist expansionism. Although massive retaliation was eventually discredited, nuclear threats, as a component of deterrence, were used again in international crises such as the Cuban Missile Crisis and the 1973 Yom Kippur War.

In terms of the balance of power, the Korean War motivated the Western powers to view Communism as an imminent threat to their security and take a more determined stance against its expansion. The USA mobilized meaningfully to enforce containment throughout the world. As the Soviet Union strove to match this impressive military build-up, Western rearmament set the tone for the arms races that marked the remainder of the Cold War. The size of the American armed forces multiplied. Massive programs for new ships, missiles, tanks, and aircraft were implemented. In Europe, England and France also increased the size of their armed forces. NATO was greatly strengthened through the establishment of unified command with strong military forces under its authority. Moreover, the impetus had been created to rearm West Germany as a part of NATO, which would actually occur in 1955.

Outside Europe, the USA ceased neglecting east Asia in its geostrategic planning. The Japan–US Security Treaty facilitated the long-term stationing of formidable American air, ground, and naval forces in Japan. Additionally, increased American military spending in Japan during the Korean War helped it on the path to economic recovery. With its relatively secure island status, large population, and growing economy, Japan became the centerpiece of American security architecture in east Asia. The USA also took greater interest in the defense of Taiwan. In the Taiwan offshore islands crises of 1954–55 and 1958, the USA appeared willing to defend Nationalist territory against Communist encroachment. But the Korean War also caused the USA to embrace global containment and the precepts of NSC 68 too tightly. In Indochina, the USA was paying for 80 percent of France's military operations by 1954. With the losses of Korea fresh in mind, Eisenhower would not send military

forces to fight the Viet Minh, nor would he agree to use nuclear weapons to save the French at Dien Ben Phu. Later administrations were less cautious and believed that the ultimate success of the Korean War in halting Communism meant that the USA would also be successful in a war in Vietnam.

The growth of American power in east Asia was inhibited by the emergence of the PRC as a military power in the region. The world now viewed the PRC as a major Communist military power and not a backward agricultural state. The Chinese military had proven that they could contend with the best forces of the West. The catastrophic defeat of the US Eighth Army in November and December 1950 showed that liberating Communist countries could be excessively dangerous. After the defeat, the USA never again tried to liberate a Communist state by invasion. For example, in the Vietnam War, the USA would not invade North Vietnam for fear of Chinese intervention. The PRC enjoyed increased influence in east Asia and the Third World. Its veteran officers became advisors in numerous national liberation movements, particularly in Vietnam. Mistakenly, the USA predominantly treated China as the unswerving and unpredictably dangerous ally of the Soviet Union. In fact, the PRC was denied entry into the UN until Nixon's presidency.

The Korean War also had implications for China's relationship with the Soviet Union. In the short term, fighting the USA reinforced the Sino-Soviet Alliance. The level of military and economic assistance provided during the war continued after 1953, with a tremendous amount of technology being transferred to the PRC. However, the war also caused the beginning of cracks in the alliance. The Chinese had fought the war largely on their own and were disappointed by the limited military involvement of the Soviet Union. The Soviet demand that China pay for all of the military equipment provided was particularly galling. More fundamentally, by the late 1950s, Mao found deep Soviet involvement in Chinese economic development and military affairs to be curtailing the PRC's independence. By the mid-1960s, these cracks would widen and the Sino-Soviet Alliance would break apart.

Finally, the Korean War symbolizes the superpower competition of the Cold War. It was the only occasion in the Cold War when the armed forces of the Soviet Union, the People's Republic of China, and the United States – plus the other Western powers – were regularly in direct combat with one another. Later in the Cold War, the superpowers only fought each other's proxies or client states. But in Korea, Soviet fighter pilots engaged in dogfights with American pilots, and Chinese infantry grappled with American infantry. Hundreds of thousands of men were taken prisoner, injured, or killed. Some of the most modern new weapons were utilized and the best generals of the three countries planned operations for the war. Historian William Stueck has gone so far as to describe it as a substitute for a Third World War. In any event, the Korean War brought the superpowers to the brink of world war. Less dramatically, the Korean War was the point where the differences between Communism and democracy, the Soviet Union and the USA, actually warranted major conventional warfare. The fact that the Korean War was a conflagration of this magnitude and intensity is sufficient reason that it should not be forgotten.

Bibliography

Published primary sources

Bussey, C., *Firefight at Yechon: Courage and Racism in the Korean War*, New York: Brassey's, 1991.

Kang, K., *Home was the Land of Morning Calm: A Saga of a Korean-American Family*, New York, 1995.

Paik Sun Yup, *From Pusan to Panmunjom*, Washington, DC, 1992.

Pears, M., and F. Kirkland (eds), *Korea Remembered: The RAN, ARA, and RAAF in the Korean War of 1950–1953*, Georges Heights, 1998.

Ridgway, M., *The Korean War*, New York, 1967.

Russ, M., *The Last Parallel: A Marine's War Journal*, New York, 1957.

Russ, M., *Breakout: The Chosin Reservoir Campaign, Korea 1950*, New York, 1999.

Weathersby, K., 'New Russian documents on the Korean War,' *Cold War International History Project Bulletin*, issues 6–7, winter 1995–96.

Secondary sources

Chen Jian, *China's Road to the Korean War: The Making of the Sino-American Confrontation*, New York, 1994.

Foot, R., *The Wrong War: American Policy and the Dimensions of the Korean Conflict, 1950-1953*, Ithaca, 1985.

Foot, R., 'Nuclear coercion and the ending of the Korean conflict,' *International Security*, vol. 13, winter 1988–89.

Futrell, F., *The United States Air Force in Korea*, New York, 1961.

Grey, J., *The Commonwealth Armies and the Korean War: An Alliance Study*, Manchester, 1988.

Hastings, M., *The Korean War*, New York, 1987.

O'Neill, R. J., *Australia in the Korean War, 1950–1953*, vols 1 and 2, Canberra, 1981, 1985.

Rees, D., *Korea: The Limited War*, New York, 1964.

Stueck, W., *The Korean War: An International History*, Princeton, 1995.

Tomedi, R., *No Bugles, No Drums: An Oral History of the Korean War*, New York, 1993.

Zhang Shu Guang, *Mao's Military Romanticism*, Lawrence, 1995.

Index

Other titles in the Essential Histories series

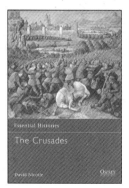

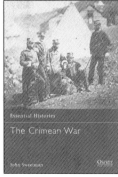

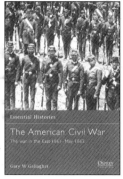

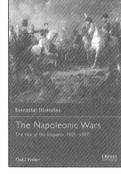

The Crusades
ISBN 1 84176 179 6

The Crimean War
ISBN 1 84176 186 9

The American Civil War
The war in the East
1861–May 1863
ISBN 1 84176 239 3

The Napoleonic Wars
The rise of the Emperor
1805–1807
ISBN 1 84176 205 9

available

available

available

available

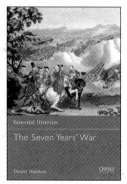

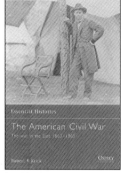

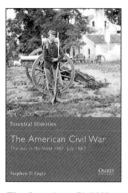

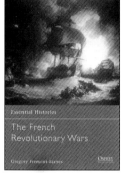

The Seven Years' War
ISBN 1 84176 191 5

The American Civil War
The war in the East
1863–1865
ISBN 1 84176 205 9

The American Civil War
The war in the West
1861–July 1863
ISBN 1 84176 240 7

**The French
Revolutionary Wars**
ISBN 1 84176 283 0

available

available

available

available

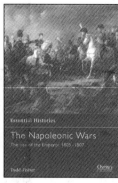

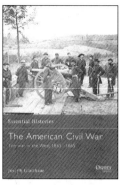

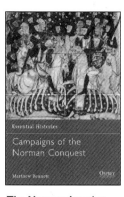

The Korean War
ISBN 1 84176 282 2

The Napoleonic Wars
The Empires fight back
1808–1812
ISBN 1 84176 298 9

The American Civil War
The war in the West
1863–1865
ISBN 1 84176 242 3

The Norman Invasion
ISBN 1 84176 228 8

available

available

November 2001

November 2001